THE

BEST LINKS
OF BRITAIN & IRELAND

Golf Course Commentaries by Nick Edmund

First published in Great Britain 2000 by
BEACON BOOKS
Koinonia House High Street Cranbrook Kent TN17 3EJ

ISBN 1 901839 19 2

©Finley Brand Communications Ltd. 2000

The moral right of the publisher has been asserted

Distributed by Grantham Book Services ‿

Cover Design by Roland Davies

Typesetting by Graphco

Printed and bound by Garzanti Verga Milan

This book may be ordered by post direct from the Publisher, but please try your book
shop first. Corporate editions and personal subscriptions of any of the Beacon Book
guides are available.
Call for details : Tel 441580 720222

Also published in the series :   **Golfing Gems of England and Wales**
                                     Golfing Gems of Scotland
                                     Golfing Gems of Ireland
                                     Golfing Gems of Florida
                                     Golfing Breaks of Britain & Ireland

Contents

Acknowledgements

We are fortunate to have many people working with us who make the task of publishing books like these a pleasure. In particular, we would like to thank Nick Edmund for his erudite prose and cheerful repudiation of deadlines. David Cannon, Mark Newcombe, Eric Hepworth and Angus McNicol for supplying such wonderful photographs. Roland Davies for his excellent design skills. The Clubs for their assistance, Karen for her cheery handling of any problems and to Daisy for her enthusiasm. To all of these people we owe our thanks but especially to you for buying the book. Thankyou.

Andrew Finley   *Robert Brand*

FOR HARRY

In the hope that you learn well the lessons that this marvellous game has to teach. In life, as in golf, there can be no mulligans. Be brave and go for your shots my son.

Andrew Finley

Foreword

*T*o adopt lawyer's jargon, it is beyond all reasonable doubt that the game of golf was invented on the east coast of Scotland. Forget those ancient Dutch and Scandinavian images of people playing a bizarre game with sticks on a frozen lake – that wasn't golf (though it may have been some bizarre form of hockey). In all probability golf began at St Andrews, on the Old Course indeed, approximately 600 years ago.

Links golf is not only the oldest, but it remains the purest and many would argue the best form of golf. (Why do you think our magazine is so named?) While there are a few authentic links courses located elsewhere in the world, by far the greater number are to be found hugging the windswept coasts of Britain and Ireland.

Attractively produced in an easy to follow format, this book serves as a wonderfully comprehensive guide to links golf in the land of its origin. Delve into its pages, then, and start planning a trip to Royal Dornoch – or Ballybunion – or Machrihanish .....

You might notice that two celebrated courses, namely Muirfield and Rye, are not included in the book; this is because they are essentially very private golf clubs. It follows, of course, that each of the 72 links courses featured do welcome visiting golfers even if unaccompanied by a club member. What a contrast to the United States! The majority of our most famous clubs are private.

If you enjoy reading LINKS Magazine, we are very confident that you will treasure your copy of 'The Best Links of Britain and Ireland.' We don't imagine it will sit on your coffee table, mind you, nor that it will be slipped into a cosy gap in your golfing library; rather we suspect it might reside somewhere very close to your passport and travel documents. If this little gem of a book doesn't inspire you to take a golfing trip to the 'Old World', nothing will.

BRAD KING

Managing Editor, LINKS Magazine

The Golf Course photographers:
David Cannon
Mark Newcombe
Eric Hepworth
Angus McNicol

Regional Introduction Photographs

England & Wales - *St Michael's Mount*
(The West Country Tourist Board)

Scotland - *Kilchurn Castle*
(The Scottish Tourist Board)

Ireland - *Powerscourt Castle*
(Bord Failte - Irish Tourist Board)

Introduction

*W*elcome to *The Best Links of Britain & Ireland*, the latest edition from Beacon Books the leading publishers of golf guides.

With the recent explosion in the number of new golf courses, all of which seem to claim that they are "championship courses" - whatever that may mean, we felt that a return to the roots of the game was well overdue.

Links land, quite literally land which links the foreshore to the mainland, was where it all began. When the only earthmoving was done with a spade, the fathers of the game took advantage of the marvellous natural contours created by shifting sand. By allowing livestock to fertilise, cut and condition the grass, some of the world's greatest courses were born. The vagaries of the wind ensure that even with modern equipment a links course will test every aspect of your game, requiring patience and imagination in equal measure.

Here then you will find a journey through the early history of the game with one or two notable recent additions. Designed to appeal to those golfers who are happy to explore new areas in their love of the game, *The Best Links* gives you 72 wonderful courses each of which, we believe, is a delight to play. Those selected have not paid for their entry, they are here on merit. Their clubhouses may not be the most luxurious, however they all offer value for money and every one is representative of the great traditions of golf, presenting a fair and testing challenge, a courteous welcome to visitors and the opportunity to savour beautiful scenery. The information supplied is concise and relevant with superb photographs to give you a feel for the course and a commentary written by Nick Edmund, one of the world's leading writers on golf courses.

Keep the guide in your car, it will become an essential companion when travelling on business or pleasure. The hotels featured have, in nearly all cases, been recommended by the relevant golf club and we feel sure that you will find them an excellent place to stay. Often the proprietors are keen golfers themselves ensuring good local knowledge and a steady supply of sympathy!

Happy golfing!

* In the Republic of Ireland some clubs express their card of the course in metres; in the editorial text, for the sake of continuity, yardages are used.

International dialling codes

From Ireland	*0044*	*(delete first 0 of local number)*
From USA	*01144*	*(delete first 0 of local number)*

England & Wales

St Michael's Mount

England & Wales

*O*verseas visitors tend to think of Scotland and Ireland before they contemplate a golfing holiday in either England or Wales. Even the great Open Championship courses in England – Royal St George's, Royal Birkdale and Royal Lytham & St Annes, plus the two no longer on the Open rota, Royal Liverpool (Hoylake) and Royal Cinque Ports are typically overlooked in the quest to play the famous Celtic courses.

Golfwise, England is arguably best known for its heathland courses – its Sunningdales and its Wentworths. Not that the essentially English powers-that-be have exactly helped the country's links reputation by selecting The Belfry near Birmingham as the venue for the last three Ryder Cups (and the next) to be played in England! It's a pity because both England and Wales really do have a marvellous selection of links courses.

There are two major centres of links golf in England, namely the Lancashire coast between Blackpool and the Wirral Peninsula, and the Kent coast between Sandwich and Deal. The former has by far the larger number of links courses for, in addition to the 'Royal trio' mentioned above (Birkdale, Lytham and Hoylake), there must be at least half a dozen first class links courses in the vicinity. Right next door to Birkdale, for instance, is Hillside, a course which in many people's opinion is every bit as good as its more celebrated neighbour. The back nine at Hillside is especially memorable. Formby, a true championship links is not far away either, while close to Hoylake is Wallasey, a delightful layout with some wonderfully undulating fairways.

Royal St George's is the 'Star of the South'. It was the first English links to host the Open Championship and today it is the only course on the Open rota within 200 miles of London. Although perhaps not in the same class as St George's (very few are), Royal Cinque Ports and Prince's certainly warrant inspection. One more to make a holiday foursome? Try Littlestone on the edge of Romney Marsh - you won't be disappointed.

Norfolk and Devon are two of southern England's quietest and most picturesque counties. Both have two exceptional yet contrasting links courses. Norfolk has Brancaster, more properly called Royal West Norfolk, and Hunstanton, while Devon has Westward Ho!, more properly called Royal North Devon, and Saunton. In addition to their royal associations, Brancaster and Westward Ho! ooze 19th century character, whereas Hunstanton and

Saunton provide more of a 'modern day' championship test. A golf holiday in Devon could be combined with a visit to Cornwall where there are two classic hidden gems: St Enodoc and West Cornwall (Lelant).

Most other English links courses appear in splendid isolation, but among those we wouldn't want you to miss are, Silloth-on-Solway in Cumbria, Hayling in Hampshire, Seaton Carew in Durham, Seacroft in Lincolnshire and Burnham and Berrow in Somerset.

And what of links golf in Wales? The two most famous courses in the Principality are undoubtedly Royal Porthcawl in the south and Royal St David's in the north. Near to each there is plenty to tempt the travelling golfer. To the west of Porthcawl are Tenby and Pennard – two unashamedly old fashioned links where blind shots and awkward stances still reign. Royal St David's is overlooked by Harlech Castle and the Snowdonia mountain range. Golfers will be spellbound by the setting of Nefyn and charmed by the quaintness of Aberdovey. Conwy and North Wales (at Llandudno) are two other fine links courses to consider when journeying to this marvellous part of the British Isles.

ABERDOVEY	ROYAL ST DAVIDS
BURNHAM & BERROW	ROYAL BIRKDALE
CONWY	ROYAL LIVERPOOL
FORMBY	ROYAL LYTHAM & ST ANNES
HAYLING	ROYAL ST GEORGE'S
HILLSIDE	ROYAL WEST NORFOLK
HUNSTANTON	SAUNTON
LITTLESTONE	SEACROFT
NEFYN	SEATON CAREW
NORTH WALES	SILLOTH ON SOLWAY
PENNARD	ST ENODOC
PRINCE'S	TENBY
ROYAL CINQUE PORTS	WALLASEY
ROYAL NORTH DEVON	WEST CORNWALL
ROYAL PORTHCAWL	

England & Wales

ST GEORGE'S CHANNEL

St Brides Bay

29

Mount's Bay

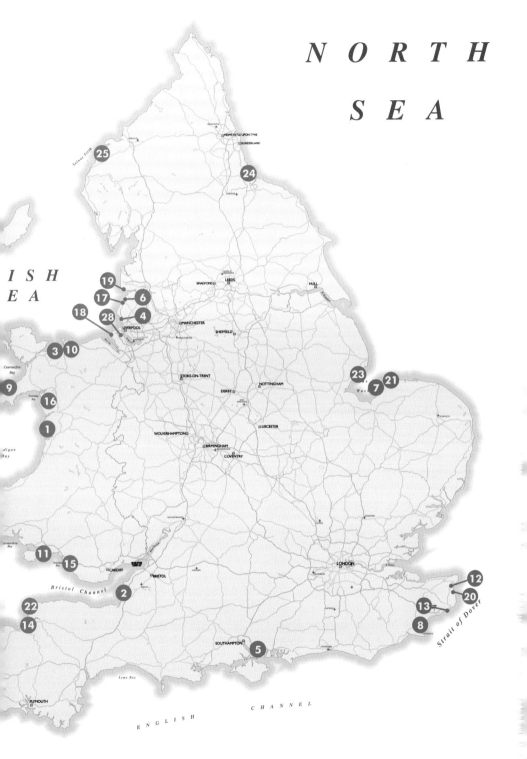

Aberdovey

*I*f golf hadn't been invented in Scotland the chances are it would have started in Aberdovey. Links golf is the most natural form of the game and nowhere does it seem so natural and harmonious a pastime as on the mouth of the Dovey estuary in western Wales. The site was so perfect for golf that when the first enthusiasts planned their course all they felt they needed to do was to purchase nine flower pots. They 'inserted' the pots into nine of the most level areas they could find and 'went golfing'. Their course occupied a thin strip of duneland, conveniently wedged between the shore and a railway line. This was back in 1892, and a romantic will tell you that not a lot has changed since.

Writing early this century, Bernard Darwin described Aberdovey as, 'the course that my soul loves best of all the courses in the world'. It is believed that Darwin's uncle was one of the pioneering 'Aberdovey flower pot men'; his great grandfather was the pioneering naturalist, Charles Darwin.

In addition to the Prestwickian railway line, Aberdovey boasts numerous old-fashioned Scottish virtues, such as capricious undulating terrain, a notorious sleepered bunker, a blind par three, and cows that graze on the links: Florida, it is not. The blind par three (actually, now no longer completely blind) is the 3rd hole and is called 'Cader'. Another classic challenge is provided by the 288 yards par four 16th – a hole that epitomises the unique character and charm of Aberdovey.

COURSE INFORMATION & FACILITIES

Aberdovey Golf Club
Aberdovey
Gwynedd LL35 0RT.

Secretary: J. M. Griffiths.
Tel: 01654 767493. Fax: 01654 767027.

Golf Professional: John Davies Tel: 01654 767602.

Green Fees:
Weekdays – £20. Weekends – £35.
Weekdays (day) – £40. Weekends (day) – £50.
Letter of introduction and handicap certificate required.
Some time restrictions. Package deals on green fees available.

CARD OF THE COURSE – PAR 71

1	2	3	4	5	6	7	8	9	Out
441	332	173	401	193	402	482	335	160	2919
Par 4	Par 4	Par 3	Par 4	Par 3	Par 4	Par 5	Par 4	Par 3	Par 34

10	11	12	13	14	15	16	17	18	In
415	407	149	530	389	477	288	428	443	3526
Par 4	Par 4	Par 3	Par 5	Par 4	Par 5	Par 4	Par 4	Par 4	Par 37

HOW TO GET THERE

[a]longside A493 immediately [t]o west of Aberdovey Village. [C]lubhouse adjacent to [ra]ilway station.

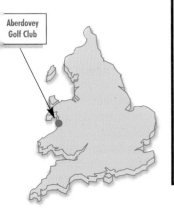

Aberdovey
Golf Club

Burnham & Berrow

*L*ittle known internationally (and indeed far from famous in Great Britain), Burnham and Berrow is one of England's finest links courses. Its lack of notoriety is due largely to its geography. Burnham and Berrow is tucked away – almost concealed – behind an ancient Iron Age fort on the coast of Somerset, a county more celebrated for its cricket than its golf. But play Burnham and Berrow and you will experience much of what is so appealing about links golf.

It is difficult to classify Burnham and Berrow in that it combines old fashioned quaintness – the odd blind shot and 'humpy bumpy' fairways – with several holes that require solid hitting and precise shot-making, a layout that's deemed strong enough and good enough to host important amateur championships. In other words, it sits somewhere between St Enodoc and Saunton.

If the links' greatest attribute is the quality and consistency of its putting surfaces, the two most visibly dominant features are the towering sand dunes, which frame many of the fairways, and the ever encroaching buckthorn-studded rough – accuracy is essential at Burnham.

There are some good holes on the front nine, notably the par threes, but it is the back nine that reveals the best and true character of Burnham. It begins with a formidable tee shot over a vast sand hill at the 10th and concludes with a tough dog-legging par four in front of the homely clubhouse.

COURSE INFORMATION & FACILITIES

Burnham & Berrow Golf Club
St Christopher's Way, Burnham-onSea,
Somerset. TA8 2PE.

Secretary: Mrs E.L.Sloman.
Tel: 01278 785760. Fax: 01278 795440.

Golf Professional Mark Crowther-Smith Tel: 01278 784545.

Green Fees:

Weekdays – £38. Weekends – £50.
Weekdays (day) – £38. Weekends (day) – £50.
Handicap certificate required. Some time restrictions.

CARD OF THE COURSE – PAR 71

1	2	3	4	5	6	7	8	9	Out
380	421	376	511	158	434	450	494	170	3394
Par 4	Par 4	Par 4	Par 5	Par 3	Par 4	Par 4	Par 5	Par 3	Par 36

10	11	12	13	14	15	16	17	18	In
375	419	401	530	192	440	344	200	445	3365
Par 4	Par 4	Par 4	Par 5	Par 3	Par 4	Par 4	Par 3	Par 4	Par 35

HOW TO GET THERE

junction 22 onto B3140 for 1.5 miles,
e left-hand turn sign posted as St
ristopher's way.

Burnham &
Berrow

Beachlands Hotel

Located in one of Weston's finest, quiet, residential areas, overlooking
the sand-dunes and 18 hole links golf course, only 300 yards level
stroll from sandy beach. Ample Private Parking, Indoor Pool &
Sauna, excellent food and 40 Malt whiskies make Beachlands Hotel
the ideal retreat from the rigours of the Golf Course!

17 Uphill Road North, Western-s-Mare,
Somerset. BS23 4NG
Telephone: 01934 621401
website: www.travel-uk.net/beachlands

Conwy

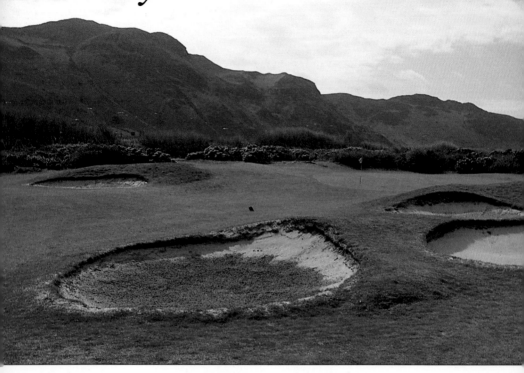

A friendly rivalry exists between the Golf Clubs of North and South Wales. Here are some of the topics of contention: 'Is Royal St David's as good as Royal Porthcawl?' 'Is Nefyn more scenic and more spectacular than Pennard?' 'Does Aberdovey possess more charm than Tenby?' And 'Is Conwy as challenging and as difficult as Ashburnham?'

So Conwy (or Caernarvonshire as it is also called) is regarded as the toughest golf course in North Wales. Laid out on the Morfa Peninsula, and originally designed by Jack Harris, Conwy is a big bear of a links. It is long – almost 7,000 yards from the championship tees – and, being generally flat, is very exposed to the elements. Much of the rough comprises thick gorse and rushes.

But Conwy has its share of beauty too (much more than Ashburnham!). From the course there are superb views of Anglesey and also of the Great Orme, towering over Llandudno. The rugged coastline around Conwy was captured on canvas in a famous series of golfing pictures by Douglas Adams, prints of which adorn clubhouses all over Britain.

Championship golf regularly comes to Conwy and in 1990 the club hosted the Home Internationals. Among the holes which test the best are the 3rd, a wonderful par four which curves along the shore and culminates in a slippery plateau green, and the 7th, a formidable two-shotter that dog-legs from left to right towards a green standing defiantly on the edge of the links, close to the beach.

COURSE INFORMATION & FACILITIES

Conwy (Caernarvonshire) Golf Club
Beacons Way
Morfa Conwy LL32 8ER.

Secretary: D.L.Brown.
Tel: 01492 592423. Fax: 01492 593363.

Golf Professional P.Lees, Tel/Fax: 01492 593225.

Green Fees:
Weekdays (Round) – £24. Weekends (Round) – £30.
Weekdays (day) – £27. Weekends (day) – £35.
Contact Secretary/Professional to book Tee times.

CARD OF THE COURSE – PAR 72

1	2	3	4	5	6	7	8	9	Out
375	147	335	393	442	177	441	435	523	3268
Par 4	Par 3	Par 4	Par 4	Par 4	Par 3	Par 4	Par 4	Par 5	Par 35

10	11	12	13	14	15	16	17	18	In
537	385	503	174	499	153	363	389	376	3379
Par 5	Par 4	Par 5	Par 3	Par 5	Par 3	Par 4	Par 4	Par 4	Par 37

HOW TO GET THERE

55 Expressway from Chester,
proceed through tunnel under
estuary, take first left, at top of
slip road turn right, follow road
to small roundabout, then turn
left to golf club.

55 Expressway from Bangor,
follow road to sign
Conwy/Marina turn left here, at
top of slip road turn left, follow
road to small
roundabout, turn
left to golf
club.

Conwy
Golf Club

Formby

*A*sk someone to describe their idea of a typical links course and the chances are they will paint a fairly bleak picture. It is likely that their course will not possess a single tree – just a dash of gorse, perhaps, and it will be very exposed to the elements. Stretching out and back, it will smile on golfers for nine holes and then blast them for the other nine. Unless, of course, this person's first thoughts are of Formby.

With sandhills aplenty, deep seaside bunkers and firm, fast fairways, Formby is certainly a links course. But Formby is also blessed with a wealth of pine trees, a feature which not only beautifies the situation, but adds a degree of protection from the wind. And Formby's routing doesn't stretch out and back, rather the bird's eye view of the links reveals eleven distinct changes in direction.

Play the 1st at Formby and you could imagine you were at Ganton, Yorkshire's celebrated 'inland links'. Gorse and heather provide a significant hazard over the opening holes as the player is drawn gradually towards the sea which, initially, is hidden behind a small forest of pines.

It is difficult to highlight individual holes, but perhaps the 3rd is the best of the early 'heathland style' challenges, while the pick of the more conventional links type holes is surely the 12th, with its superbly sited green and characterful fairway that was once described as 'billowing like a sail in a breeze.'

HOW TO GET THERE

t the Junction of the M57 &M58 take the
565 to Formby signposted. On the A565
rom the Liverpool Direction, turn left at
he scond roundabout (with BP Station)
owards formby.

Formby
Golf Club

COURSE INFORMATION & FACILITIES

Formby Golf Club
Golf Road, Formby,
Liverpool L37 1LQ

Secretary: Mr K.R.Wilcox
Tel: 01704 872164. Fax: 01704 833028.

Golf Professional Mr G.H.Butler Tel: 01704 873090.

Green Fees:
Weekdays – £60. Weekends – £60.
Weekdays (day) – £60. Weekends (day) – £60.
Handicap certificate required. Some time restrictions

CARD OF THE COURSE – PAR 72

1	2	3	4	5	6	7	8	9	Out
435	403	538	312	183	428	388	493	450	3630
Par 4	Par 4	Par 5	Par 4	Par 3	Par 4	Par 4	Par 5	Par 4	Par 37

10	11	12	13	14	15	16	17	18	In
215	422	421	431	431	403	127	494	419	3363
Par 5	Par 4	Par 4	Par 3	Par 5	Par 4	Par 3	Par 4	Par 4	Par 35

Hayling

*I*t has been called 'The poor man's Rye', but Tom Simpson, one of golf's greatest architects, once described the duneland at Hayling as, 'The best linksland in Britain'.

Founded in 1883, and very fashionable in the early part of this century, Hayling has become something of a forgotten links. Its setting is unusual rather than remote. It occupies the southern tip of Hayling Island (which is linked by road to the mainland) and stares across The Solent to the Isle of Wight. Hayling is a traditional links with firm fairways and fast greens; it is raw and rugged, although its present day moonscape appearance owes much to the fact that it was heavily bombed during the War.

The eccentric genius, Tom Simpson (you may have guessed) was largely responsible for the design of the course. A man who travelled everywhere by chauffeur driven Rolls Royce and was responsible for the amazing routing of Cruden Bay was never likely to deliver a humdrum layout, and Hayling is certainly not that. The course starts out quietly but quickly gathers momentum. The finest sequence of holes – and the most spectacular duneland – occurs between the 10th and 13th. The 10th is an interesting short par four which can be driven (a fourball once recorded scores of 1, 2, 3, and 4); the 11th is an outstanding par three with a lovely plateau green; the 12th is a mighty two-shotter running parallel to the shore, and the charming, 'up and over' 13th features a massive bunker known as 'The Widow'.

COURSE INFORMATION & FACILITIES

Hayling Golf Club
Links Lane, Hayling Island
Hampshire PO11 0BX.

Secretary: Chris Cavill.
Tel: 01705 464446.

Golf Professional Ray Gadd Tel: 01705 464491.

Green Fees:

Weekdays – £28. Weekends – £35.
Weekdays (day) – £33. Weekends (day) – £45.
Handicap certificate required. Some time restrictions.

CARD OF THE COURSE – PAR 71

1	2	3	4	5	6	7	8	9	Out
179	495	398	410	163	434	505	352	414	3350
Par 3	Par 5	Par 4	Par 4	Par 3	Par 4	Par 5	Par 4	Par 4	Par 36

10	11	12	13	14	15	16	17	18	In
270	157	444	341	534	430	178	432	385	3171
Par 4	Par 3	Par 4	Par 4	Par 5	Par 4	Par 3	Par 4	Par 4	Par 35

HOW TO GET THERE

...om M27, (A3(M) and A27. Leave the A27
...the Havant/Hayling Island Junction and
...llow the main road (A3023) over
...ngstone Bridge onto the Island.
...ntinue to roundabout, take second exit.
...ntinue 1 mile to roundabout, take
...cond exit. After 3/4 mile entrance is on
...t opposite Sinah Lane.

Hayling Golf Club

Newtown House Hotel
Hayling Island

An "OASIS" in a world full of Chaos.

*After a tiring day on the golf course soothe your weary bones in our
"New Wave" leisure complex which consists of a sauna, steam room,
jacuzzi and an indoor swimming pool.*

*Come and relax in the atmosphere of our "Olde Worlde" hotel.
Enjoy the good fayre, wine and ale as served by us.*

**Newtown House Hotel
Manor Road, Hayling Island, Hants PO11 0QR
Tel: 023 92 466131 · Fax: 023 92 461366**

23

Hillside

he east coast of Scotland is where golf began; the Ayrshire coast is where the Open Championship was born and yet, history aside, many believe that the greatest stretch of linksland in the British Isles is to be found on the Lancashire coast of north west England. Between Liverpool and Blackpool, a distance of 40 miles, lie a string of golfing pearls. Royal Birkdale stands proudly in the middle of this region and immediately adjacent to Birkdale is Hillside, a truly marvellous links.

In terms of international stature, Hillside is overshadowed by its illustrious neighbour – this despite the fact that it has staged many major amateur events and, in 1982, the PGA Championship. In terms of challenge, however, Hillside is every bit as good as Birkdale. The terrain is similar, of course, with massive dunes and deep bunkers the dominant features.

Hillside's strengths are the quality of its par fives and the spectacular, rollercoasting nature of its back nine – once described as being 'like Ballybunion minus the Atlantic Ocean'. The best of the early holes are the 3rd, an excellent dog-leg, and the par five 5th which features a highly unusual cross bunker. The back nine begins with an outstanding short hole played uphill to a green practicallly encircled by gaping traps. It is from here on that Hillside resembles Ballybunion. The two par fives, the 11th and 17th, are the most dramatic holes, their fairways twisting and turning along magnificent dune-lined valleys.

COURSE INFORMATION & FACILITIES

Hillside Golf Club
The Club House, Hastings Road
Hillside, Southport, Merseyside PR8 2LU.

Secretary: J. G. Graham.
Tel: 01704 567169. Fax: 01704 563192.

Golf Professional Brian Seddon Tel: 01704 568360.

Green Fees:
Weekdays – £45. Weekends – £60.
Weekdays (day) – £60.
Handicp certificate required. Some time restrictions.
Tuesday, ladies day till 2pm. No play Satuarday.
Limited Sunday.

CARD OF THE COURSE – PAR 72

1	2	3	4	5	6	7	8	9	Out
399	525	402	195	504	413	176	405	425	3444
Par 4	Par 5	Par 4	Par 3	Par 5	Par 4	Par 3	Par 4	Par 4	Par 36

10	11	12	13	14	15	16	17	18	In
147	508	368	398	400	398	199	548	440	3406
Par 3	Par 5	Par 4	Par 4	Par 4	Par 4	Par 3	Par 5	Par 4	Par 36

HOW TO GET THERE

3 miles south of the centre of Southport on the A565 o Liverpool.

Hillside
Golf Club

Hunstanton

*C*linging to the Norfolk coastline and routinely buffeted by strong winds are two classic English links courses: Royal West Norfolk (or Brancaster to give its more popular name) and Hunstanton (occasionally pronounced 'Hunston').

Hunstanton is renowned for its slick 'marble stair case' like greens, and for its often deep, strategically positioned bunkers. Like Brancaster, the course runs 'out and back', although not rigidly so, rather it meanders away from the clubhouse, reaches the 8th green, and meanders its way home. The outward holes have the River Hun for company – invariably it is off to the right – and the inward ones are laid out closer to the shore. At first glance the links looks fairly flat, and indeed there aren't any major climbs up or down, but the course has more than its fair share of subtle undulations and there are a number of elevated tees and plateau greens, some of which offer extensive views of both sea and country.

If the spectacularly bunkered short 7th and the long par four 11th with its ever-narrowing valley fairway are the finest holes at Hunstanton, then the most celebrated, or rather the one that has given most cause for celebration, is undoubtedly the par three 16th. In 1974 a player named Robert Taylor holed his tee shot here on three successive days! Taylor used a 1-iron on the first day (into the wind) and a 6-iron on the second and third day. Presumably he was a shade miffed when he missed the hole on day four!

COURSE INFORMATION & FACILITIES

Hunstanton Golf Club
Golf Course Road, Old Hunstanton,
Norfolk. PE36 6JQ

Secretary: Malcolm Whybrow
Tel: 01485 532811. Fax: 01485 532319.

Golf Professional John Carter Tel: 01485 532751.

Green Fees:
Weekdays (day) – £50. Weekends (day) – £60. After 4pm
Weekdays (round) – £30. Weekends (round) – £40.
Handicap certificate required. Some time restrictions

CARD OF THE COURSE – PAR 72

1	2	3	4	5	6	7	8	9	Out
343	532	443	172	436	337	166	505	513	3237
Par 4	Par 5	Par 4	Par 3	Par 4	Par 4	Par 3	Par 5	Par 5	Par 37

10	11	12	13	14	15	16	17	18	In
375	439	358	387	219	478	189	445	398	3096
Par 4	Par 4	Par 4	Par 4	Par 3	Par 5	Par 3	Par 4	Par 4	Par 35

HOW TO GET THERE

mile North of Hunstanton.
rn off A149 in village of Old Hunstanton
gnposted).

Hunstanton
Golf Club

Littlestone

The most commonly adopted description of Littlestone is 'overshadowed' - its qualities kept in the shade by the brighter and greater reputations of Royal St George's, Deal and Prince's, all situated further east along the Kent coast. But then Littlestone was never destined to be famous, for its location, adjacent to Romney Marsh is both stark and remote. There is an almost medieval feel to this part of Kent - an ancient, forgotten land.

Littlestone Golf Club was founded in 1888. The course was initially designed by Laidlaw Purves and revised by James Braid early this century. Although the site does incorporate an impressive range of sandhills, the course is essentially quite flat and, consequently, uneven lies and awkward stances are rarely encountered. What determines a player's strategy at Littlestone is the course's expert bunkering and the strength and direction of the wind: what you see (and feel !) at Littlestone is what you get.

The course opens benignly with a short, straightaway par four. This is followed by a testing two-shotter, but in truth the first six holes are mere appetisers. The sequence from the 7th to the 11th is full of variety and interest while the two most outstanding holes are undoubtedly the 16th and 17th. The former is a long, uphill, dog-legging par four with an elusive green that is both raised and heavily contoured; as for the 17th, it is a classic links par three, its green blending into a wonderfully natural dune setting.

HOW TO GET THERE

om Junction 10 on M20
ke A2070 to Brenzett.
259 to New Romney – turn
ght on B2071 to Littlestone.
ter 1¼ miles turn left in
adeira Rd. The clubhouse
to your left front after
00 yds.

Littlestone
Golf Club

COURSE INFORMATION & FACILITIES

Littlestone Golf Club
St. Andrews Road, Littlestone,
New Romney, Kent TN28 8RB.
Secretary: Colonel Charles Moorhouse.
Tel: 01797 363355.   Fax: 01l797 362740.
Golf Professional Tel: 01797 362231.
Green Fees:
Weekdays – £28. Weekends – £45.
Weekdays (days) £39. Weekends (day) £50.
Restrictions: Very little scope for weekend visitors.

CARD OF THE COURSE – PAR 71

1	2	3	4	5	6	7	8	9	Out
297	410	392	370	491	157	507	385	175	3184
Par 4	Par 4	Par 4	Par 4	Par 5	Par 3	Par 5	Par 4	Par 3	Par 36

10	11	12	13	14	15	16	17	18	In
413	372	393	411	183	359	468	179	498	3276
Par 4	Par 4	Par 4	Par 4	Par 3	Par 4	Par 4	Par 3	Par 5	Par 35

Nefyn & District

Which is the most scenic seaside course in England and Wales? A shortlist of five might include the following: East Devon, The Isle of Purbeck, Pennard, Bamburgh Castle and Nefyn & District. Most first time visitors to Nefyn are left spellbound by the beauty of its setting and vow to return at the earliest opportunity.

Situated on the Lleyn Peninsula of north west Wales, Nefyn is essentially a clifftop course but is very 'linksy' in parts. There are some large sand hills in the middle of the course, and occasionally players are asked to fire a shot over the dunes, but for much of the round the course runs along the top of the cliffs – an exhilarating, if potentially perilous journey!

Measuring a little over 6500 yards from the back markers, Nefyn is not the longest of challenges, although when the wind blows it can, of course, be very tricky. On calm days, with the sea visible from every hole, it is a classic holiday course and the relaxed atmosphere at the nineteenth hole enhances this mood.

After a downhill par four opening hole, the course hugs the edge of the cliffs for a spectacular series of holes; it then turns back on itself before heading off in a different direction out on to a headland where perhaps the best holes of all, numbers 11 to 18 are found. In a sandy cove just below the 12th green (and, we are told, accessible from the course), is the Ty Coch Inn. Well, if the holiday mood really takes you...

COURSE INFORMATION & FACILITIES

Nefyn & District Golf Club
Morfa Nefyn
Gwynedd LL53 6DA.

Secretary: Mr. J. B. Owens.
Tel: 01758 720966. Fax: 01758 720476.

Golf Professional Mr J Froom Tel: 01758 720102.

Green Fees per 18 holes per day:
Weekdays – £25. Weekends – £30.
Weekdays (day) – £30. Weekends (day) – £35.
Handicap certificate required. Some time restrictions.

CARD OF THE COURSE (New) – PAR 71

1	2	3	4	5	6	7	8	9	Out
458	374	397	477	156	442	401	327	166	3198
Par 4	Par 4	Par 4	Par 5	Par 3	Par 4	Par 4	Par 4	Par 3	Par 35

10	11	12	13	14	15	16	17	18	In
415	181	349	344	401	405	367	512	376	3350
Par 4	Par 3	Par 4	Par 4	Par 4	Par 4	Par 4	Par 5	Par 4	Par 36

HOW TO GET THERE

Nefyn & District Golf Club is situated on the Lleyn Peninsula. It is approached from the north on the A499 and B4417 through Nefyn and from the south the A497 through to Morfa Nefyn.

Nefyn & District Golf Club

North Wales

*A*lice Liddell, the girl who inspired Lewis Carroll to write Alice in Wonderland, spent 'the golden years of her childhood' on the sands of Llandudno's West Shore. Today golfers playing at North Wales try their level best to avoid visiting the same beach.

Founded in 1894, North Wales is one of two fine courses in Llandudno. The more widely known (and possibly more difficult) is Llandudno Measdu; however, for connossieurs of traditional links golf, North Wales may hold greater appeal. For one thing, it is an exceptionally scenic course – the Welsh coastline is at its most dramatic around Llandudno; it also possesses enormous character with humpy, hillocky fairways, awkward stances and the occasional blind shot.

Heather and gorse lurk immediately beyond the fairways and several of the greens are defended by deep bunkers.

The links begins rather modestly but quickly plunges into some exciting duneland. The first outstanding hole at North Wales is the 5th, a par five that dog-legs into the wind along a rollercoasting, bottle-neck shaped fairway. Two of the best par fours are the 8th, where you journey through a narrow valley menaced by a railway line and the beach, and the Stroke One 11th which runs uphill into the wind, and where the beach again threatens. As for the par threes holes, the finest is the 16th: 'O.L.' it is called – a cry you may utter should your tee shot land in the deep bunker to the left of this partially hidden, bowl shaped green.

COURSE INFORMATION & FACILITIES

North Wales Golf Club (Llandudno)
72 Brynian Road, West Shore,
Llandudno, Conwy LL30 2DZ.

Secretary: W.Roger Williams.
Tel: 01492 875325. Fax: 01492 873355.

Golf Professional: Richard Bradbury Tel: 01492
876878. Fax: 01492 872420

Green Fees:
Weekdays – £18. Weekends – £23.
Weekdays (day) – £25. Weekends (day) – £35.
Some time restrictions.

CARD OF THE COURSE – PAR 71

1	2	3	4	5	6	7	8	9	Out
344	359	338	200	510	385	498	387	347	3368
Par 4	Par 4	Par 4	Par 3	Par 5	Par 4	Par 5	Par 4	Par 4	Par 37

10	11	12	13	14	15	16	17	18	In
400	420	359	182	530	334	151	120	383	2874
Par 4	Par 4	Par 4	Par 3	Par 5	Par 4	Par 3	Par 3	Par 4	Par 33

HOW TO GET THERE

avelling from Chester to North
ales Golf Club, do not turn off A470
 Llandudno take the next exit signed
 nwy/Deganwy over railway line
 st "Tesco" on left then take A546 to
 ganwy stay on main road for
 proximately one mile (passing
 esdu Golf Club-house on the right)
 er railway bridge and North Wales
 lf Club is on the left.

North Wales
Golf Club

Pennard

*F*ounded around the turn of the century, and originally laid out by James Braid, Pennard has long enjoyed a reputation as 'Wales' best kept golfing secret'. Tom Doak, a leading American golf course architect and controversial course critic has threatened to let the proverbial cat out of the bag by describing it (in his book The Confidential Guide to Golf Courses) as 'One of my all-time favourites', adding, 'the site is one of the most spectacular I've ever seen'.

As usual, Doak is spot on: Pennard is indeed a jewel of a links. It is to be found on the Gower Peninsula, just beyond the little village of Pennard. The course is essentially a links, although, rather like Royal Porthcawl,

much of it lies on high ground, on this occasion overlooking the great sandy sweeps of Oxwich Bay and Three Cliff Bay. Delightfully old-fashioned, or as Doak puts it, 'awful quirky', Pennard is not a long course but nonetheless provides a stern challenge. The links is routinely buffeted by strong winds that roar up the Bristol Channel and much of the rough consists of thick gorse and rust coloured bracken.

The hole that everyone remembers at Pennard is the short par four 7th. Here you drive over a deep valley to find a fairway which runs alongside the ruins of a 12th century Norman castle; you then pitch to a partially concealed, sunken green – a quirky golf hole, if ever there was one.

rom M4 - Junction 42 eight
miles west of Swansea via
483 and A4067. Turn right
t The Woodman Inn -
lackPill and take B4436 to
ennard.

Pennard
Golf Club

COURSE INFORMATION & FACILITIES

Pennard Golf Club
2 Southgate Road, Southgate,
Swansea SA3 2BT.

Secretary: Morley Howell.
Tel: 01792 233131. Fax: 01792 233457.

Golf Professional M.V.Bennett Tel: 01792 233451.

Green Fees:
Weekdays – £24. Weekends – £30 (Bank Holidays).
Handicap certificate required. Some time restrictions.
Societies week-days only.

CARD OF THE COURSE – PAR 71

1	2	3	4	5	6	7	8	9	Out
449	145	365	517	165	400	351	357	437	3186
Par 4	Par 3	Par 4	Par 5	Par 3	Par 4	Par 4	Par 4	Par 4	Par 35

10	11	12	13	14	15	16	17	18	In
492	180	298	196	368	165	493	488	399	3079
Par 5	Par 3	Par 4	Par 3	Par 4	Par 3	Par 5	Par 5	Par 4	Par 36

Prince's

You think of Prince's and you think of the late Gene Sarazen. 'The Squire', as he was affectionately known, was the first golfer to win all four of the game's Major championships; he was the player who 'made' the Masters when he holed a four wood for an albatross two at the 15th en route to winning at Augusta in 1935; at the ripe old age of 71 he holed-in-one at the 8th, the famous 'Postage Stamp', during the 1973 Open Championship at Troon, and it was Sarazen who won the Championship in 1932 on the one occasion it was held at Prince's.

Situated 'next door' to Royal St George's on the Kent coast at Sandwich, Prince's has the kind of geography and terrain that made it an ideal site for war time manoeuvres; indeed in the immediate post war years there was talk of Prince's becoming a permanent military training base. But, happily for golfers, in 1950 the links was restored to its former glory – although not as an 18 hole Championship course, rather as a layout comprising 27 holes, the present day three loops of nine.

With windswept plateaued greens, rippling fairways and tangling rough, each of the nines at Prince's (the Himalayas, Shore and Dunes) presents a daunting test of traditional links golf. It is hard to say which is the best nine but a selection of the finest holes might include the 2nd, 7th and 8th from the Himalayas, the 3rd, 6th and 9th from the Shore and the 3rd, 4th and 6th from the Dunes.

COURSE INFORMATION & FACILITIES

Prince's Golf Club
Sandwich Bay, Sandwich
Kent CT13 9QB.

Secretary: Mr W.M.Howie.
Tel: 01304 611118. Fax: 01304 612000.

Golf Professional Derick Barbour
Tel: 01304 613797. Fax: 01304 612000

Green Fees per 18 holes per day:
Weekdays – £42. Weekends: – £47 (Sat), £50 (Sun).
Weekdays (day) – £50. Weekends (day) – £55 (Sat/Sun).

CARD OF THE COURSE (Shore/Dunes)

1	2	3	4	5	6	7	8	9	Out
420	485	161	385	377	393	538	176	412	3347
Par 4	Par 5	Par 3	Par 4	Par 4	Par 4	Par 5	Par 3	Par 4	Par 36

10	11	12	13	14	15	16	17	18	In
440	147	484	400	406	487	363	200	416	3343
Par 4	Par 3	Par 5	Par 4	Par 4	Par 5	Par 4	Par 3	Par 4	Par 36

HOW TO GET THERE

A25, A2, M2, A2, A256 to
Sandwich.
Turn right into St George's
Road before 'Elf' service
station, then right into
Sandown Road, through
Tollgate into Sandwich Bay
Estate, then left into Kings
Avenue, turn left at Seafront
and continue
along to
Prince's.

Prince's
Golf Club

Royal Birkdale

*F*or a club whose origins were very humble, Royal Birkdale has enjoyed a remarkable 20th century. Founded in 1889, the club's first course was a modest nine hole layout on land rented from the local council. Even when it moved to its present home in 1897 things got off to an unceremonious start when the members' clubhouse had to be pulled down on discovery that it had been built on someone else's land!

There have been two especially significant decades in the 20th century, namely the 1930s and the 1960s. It was in the thirties that the celebrated links we know today essentially took shape, courtesy of Fred Hawtree and John H Taylor. The club's striking art deco clubhouse was also built in this era.

The sixties were truly halcyon days. Between 1961 and 1971 Birkdale hosted three Opens and two Ryder Cups. The decade began with Arnold Palmer slashing his way through strong winds to win a first British Open, and ended with Lee Trevino wise-cracking all the way to his first Championship success. In between, Jack Nicklaus conceded Tony Jacklin's three foot putt, and the two shook hands on a Ryder Cup tie.

The professionals love Birkdale. Although every hole is framed by spectacular dunes, the fairways are quite flat, thus blind shots and awkward stances are almost non-existent. The greatest holes are thought by many to be the demanding 6th and the short 12th – 'one of the world's finest par threes', according to Tom Watson.

COURSE INFORMATION & FACILITIES

Royal Birkdale Golf Club
Waterloo Road, Birkdale,
Southport. PR8 2LX

Secretary: M.C.Gilveat
Tel: 01704 567920.

Golf Professional R.N.Bradbeer Tel: 01704 567920.

Green Fees:
Weekdays – £98. Weekends – £125.
Weekdays (day) – £125.
Handicap certificate required. Some time restrictions.

CARD OF THE COURSE – PAR 70

1	2	3	4	5	6	7	8	9	Out
449	421	407	203	344	473	177	457	411	3342
Par 4	Par 4	Par 4	Par 3	Par 4	Par 5	Par 3	Par 4	Par 4	Par 34

10	11	12	13	14	15	16	17	18	In
403	408	183	475	198	544	416	547	472	3646
Par 4	Par 4	Par 3	Par 4	Par 3	Par 5	Par 4	Par 5	Par 4	Par 36

HOW TO GET THERE

From M6 junction 31 A59/A565 Southport
follow signs to Liverpool or junction 26
A58 to Ormskirk A570 to Southport then
town centre A565 to Liverpool.
From M62 junction 6 M57 to Bootle, A565
Southport.

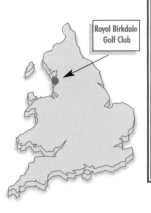

Royal Birkdale
Golf Club

Royal Cinque Ports

R oyal Cinque Ports, or Deal as it is better known, is situated just a few miles along the coast from Royal St George's. Deal may not possess the spectacular ruggedness of Royal St George's, nor its extraordinary feeling of spaciousness, but what Deal does have, is some of the finest and best maintained putting surfaces in the British Isles.

Two Open Championships have been held at Deal, the first in 1909 and a second in 1920. The 1909 Championship was won by John H Taylor, the fourth of his five victories, and in 1920 Abe Mitchell allowed George Duncan to come from 13 strokes behind to snatch an unlikely victory. Plans to stage a third Open at Deal in 1949 had to be abandoned when extensive flooding forced a temporary closure of the course.

Deal is an exposed links and very often it is Mother Nature that provides the greatest challenge. Strong winds, billowing in from the sea, and capable of changing direction several times during a round, can turn seemingly modest holes into monsters. The fairways are humpy and hillocky and well bunkered. Many of the greens sit on natural plateaux.

While the first four holes at Deal are full of variety, it is the back nine that is the more demanding and generally more interesting of the two halves. The finish is quite fearsome and, in the 16th, includes one of the most classical links holes in golf.

COURSE INFORMATION & FACILITIES

Royal Cinque Ports Golf Club
Golf Road, Deal,
Kent. CT14 6RF

Secretary: Mr Colin Hammond
Tel: 01304 374007. Fax: 01304 379530.

Golf Professional Andrew Reynolds Tel/Fax: 01304 374170

Green Fees:
Weekdays – £50. (After 1pm).
Weekdays (day) – £60.
Handicap certificate required. Some time restrictions.
Society packages available.

CARD OF THE COURSE – PAR 72

1	2	3	4	5	6	7	8	9	Out
357	399	489	150	501	314	381	166	410	3167
Par 4	Par 4	Par 5	Par 3	Par 5	Par 4	Par 4	Par 3	Par 4	Par 36

10	11	12	13	14	15	16	17	18	In
364	401	440	423	223	447	508	371	410	3433
Par 4	Par 4	Par 4	Par 4	Par 3	Par 4	Par 5	Par 4	Par 4	Par 36

HOW TO GET THERE

20 motorway to Dover:
258 to Deal. Continue along Sea Front
ea on right hand side) until road turns
ft into Godwyn Road. Turn right at end of
odwyn Road (T junction) into Golf Road,
ubhouse is about 500 yards along on the
ft hand side.

Royal Cinque
Ports Golf Club

Royal Liverpool

A long with Royal St George's, Royal Liverpool is probably England's most famous and most traditional golf club. Established in 1869, its links course at Hoylake is the country's second oldest after Westward Ho!, although it hasn't always been such an exclusive venue. In its early days the club had to share the links with a racecourse, and hoofprints on the fairways were a common hazard! Fortunately by 1876 the horses had found elsewhere to gallop and a century and a quarter later the club can pride itself on having hosted 10 Open Championships and 17 British Amateur Championships.

No club in the world has a greater record or stronger ties with major amateur golf. Britain's two finest amateur golfers,

John Ball and Harold Hilton, who between them won 12 British Amateur titles and three Open Championships, both played their early golf at Hoylake. And in 1930 the greatest amateur golfer of all time, Bobby Jones, won the second leg of his historic Grand Slam at Royal Liverpool.

An impressive clubhouse overlooks a golf course which, at first glance anyway, appears unimpressive. Hoylake, like St Andrews, demands closer inspection. The terrain is generally flat (except at the far end of the links) but the layout is brimful of subtlety and strategy. Hoylake's principal hazards – aside from an ever-present wind – are its superbly placed bunkers and, rather unusually, its Out-of-Bounds, a feature that introduces itself on the opening hole.

HOW TO GET THERE

oyal Liverpool Golf Club is situated on
eols Drive (A540) between Hoylake and
est Kirby, 10 minutes from Junction 2 of
e M53 and less than 1 hour from
anchester International Airport. We are
se to Hoylake railway station
erseytravel line).

Royal Liverpool
Golf Club

COURSE INFORMATION & FACILITIES

Royal Liverpool Golf Club
Meols Drive, Hoylake,
Wirral CH47 4AZ

Secretary: Group Captain C.T Moore CBE
Tel: 0151 6323101. Fax: 0151 6326737.

Golf Professional John Heggarty Tel: 0151 6325868.

Green Fees:
Weekdays – £60. Weekends – £100.
Weekdays (day) – £85.
Letter of introduction and Handicap certificate required.
Some time restrictions.

CARD OF THE COURSE – PAR 72

1	2	3	4	5	6	7	8	9	Out
429	393	505	194	448	422	198	519	392	3500
Par 4	Par 4	Par 5	Par 3	Par 4	Par 4	Par 3	Par 5	Par 4	Par 36

10	11	12	13	14	15	16	17	18	In
412	200	455	159	547	459	558	420	418	3628
Par 4	Par 3	Par 4	Par 3	Par 5	Par 4	Par 5	Par 4	Par 4	Par 36

Royal Lytham & St Annes

*I*f British links courses were rated
solely on their aesthetic merits, Royal
Lytham wouldn't score too highly.
Nor would Lytham fare particularly well if
they were judged according to their
proximity to the sea. The Lancashire links
is situated about a mile from the coast and
is surrounded by red brick suburbia. You
won't see an equivalent of Ailsa Craig or
Bass Rock here, but you will glimpse
Blackpool Tower and a busy commuter
railway line.

Fortunately golf isn't a beauty contest.
And when our links courses are assessed in
terms of challenge, character and history,
Royal Lytham sits very near the top of any
list.

To play at Royal Lytham is to tread on
hallowed ground. This is the links
immortalised by Bobby Jones and twice

conquered by Seve Ballesteros. It is where
Gary Player putted left-handed from up
against the clubhouse walls, and where
Tony Jacklin rifled that arrow-straight
drive down the 18th to become the first
'British' Open champion in 18 years.

Royal Lytham is rich in tradition and
strong on golf architecture, albeit that it is
rather non-conformist - beginning with a
par three hole, and including back-to-back
par fives on the front nine. Lytham is also
a bit lop-sided. The back nine invariably
plays much longer and tougher than the
front nine. The finishing sequence,
however, is legendary. To be especially
savoured are the 17th, where in the 1926
Open, Jones hit one of the most
sensational shots in golfing history, and the
18th, one of the game's truly great
finishing holes.

HOW TO GET THERE

...ction 31 (M6) to M55. Continue to end.
...nore early signs for Lytham St Annes).
...low signs at end of motorway to Lytham
...Annes. This will take you to Squires
...te Lane (Airport sign), after passing
...port continue over railway bridge to
...ton Drive North (A548) after passing
...ough St Annes turn
... into St Thomas'
...ad, Golf
...rse is
...r the
...lway
...dge,
...t right.

Royal Lytham &
St Annes
Golf Club

COURSE INFORMATION & FACILITIES

Royal Lytham & St Annes Golf Club
Links Gate,Lytham St Annes,
Lancashire. FY8 3LQ

Secretary: Lytton B Goodwin
Tel: 01253 780946. Fax: 01253 724206.

Golf Professional Eddie Birchenough Tel: 01253 720094.

Green Fees:
Weekdays – £90.
Handicap certificate required. Some time restrictions.
Visitors on Mondays & Thursdays only.
Green fee includes lunch.

CARD OF THE COURSE – PAR 71

1	2	3	4	5	6	7	8	9	Out
206	420	458	393	188	486	551	406	162	3270
Par 3	Par 4	Par 4	Par 4	Par 3	Par 5	Par 5	Par 4	Par 3	Par 35

10	11	12	13	14	15	16	17	18	In
334	485	189	339	445	468	356	413	386	3415
Par 4	Par 5	Par 3	Par 4	Par 4	Par 4	Par 4	Par 4	Par 4	Par 36

Royal North Devon

*I*magine. You are on the 1st tee of the first 'Royal' golf club you have ever played. Slightly nervously, you tee up your ball then take a few paces backwards to survey the fairway ahead. Just as you try to visualise your opening drive a sheep wanders up to your ball; it bleats a couple of times before strolling leisurely to the edge of the teeing area. There is only one place you could be.

The links at Westward Ho! is a very special place. This is the home of the Royal North Devon Golf Club, the oldest English club still playing over its original land (since 1864) and the home of the oldest ladies' golf club in the world (established in 1868). And it is surely the only golf course in the world –

never mind 'Royal Club' – where the above episode is a distinct possibility.

The 18 holes are situated on Northam Burrows, a vast and very exposed area of common land which stretches along the coast just to the north of Bideford. It is an extraordinary piece of terrain. In places it is pancake flat; in other parts the fairways ripple and undulate in a manner reminiscent of St Andrews. The hazards comprise an interesting mix of ditches, pot bunkers and, at the far end of the links, the Great Sea Rushes – giant marshland reeds unique to Westward Ho! and which can literally impale golf balls. There is also the famous sleepered Cape Bunker at the 4th which is at least 100 yards wide and quite intimidating to drive over.

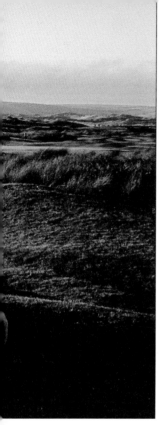

COURSE INFORMATION & FACILITIES

Royal North Devon Golf Club
Golf Links Road, Westward Ho!
Bideford, Devon EX39 1HD.
Secretary: Robert Fowler.
Tel: 01237 473817. Fax: 01237 423456.

Golf Professional Richard Herring
Tel: 01237 477598. Fax: 01237 423456

Green Fees:
Weekdays – £30. Weekends – £36.
Weekdays (day) – £36. Weekends (day) – £40.
Handicap certificates required. Some time restrictions.

CARD OF THE COURSE – PAR 72

1	2	3	4	5	6	7	8	9	Out
478	416	421	349	136	406	397	192	497	3292
Par 5	Par 4	Par 4	Par 4	Par 3	Par 4	Par 4	Par 3	Par 5	Par 36

10	11	12	13	14	15	16	17	18	In
373	371	423	442	201	439	143	555	414	3361
Par 4	Par 4	Par 4	Par 4/5	Par 3	Par 4	Par 3	Par 5	Par 4	Par 36

HOW TO GET THERE

5 Junction 27 onto A361. Follow to
rnstaple picking up A39 to Bideford –
oss new bridge over River Torridge turn
ght at roundabout following signs to
estward Ho!/Appledore and Northam.
st before entering Westward Ho! Take
rning right into Beach Road and turn
ght at bottom of road
o Golf Links Road
d the Golf
ub is
ong on
ur left.

Royal North Devon
Golf Club

THE MOUNT
G U E S T   H O U S E

AA
★★★★

We welcome you to The Mount. This small interesting Georgian building is full of character and
charm. It is set in a semi-walled and private garden with large and handsome trees, making it a
peaceful haven so close to the town centre.

All six bedrooms have been tastefully decorated and furnished. They are all en suite and equipped
with colour televisions. A recent addition is a ground floor bedroom which is a particular
advantage for those guests to whom stairs are a problem.

The town centre of Bidford is only a short walk away. It is an historic and interesting town with its
quay, narrow streets and medieval bridges.

We are only 5 minutes drive from the Royal North Devon Golf Club - the oldest golf course in
England. (Discounted green fees available).

Royal Porthcawl

On a calm day Royal Porthcawl looks a pussycat of a links. Where are the towering sand dunes of Birkdale, the rollercoasting fairways of Sandwich and the gaping bunkers of Carnoustie? But play Porthcawl on a rough day and you will not harbour such thoughts. In 1995 the club hosted the Walker Cup and at times the weather was foul. Young Master Woods and his US team mates failed to cope with the conditions as Great Britain and Ireland gained a famous victory. A pussycat of a links? Porthcawl humbled 'the Tiger'.

The layout is spectacular in scenic terms – every hole provides a view of the sea – but the absence of large dunes causes people to underestimate the challenge. Porthcawl is very exposed to the elements, moreover, the hazards are intelligently placed and full of variety.

Porthcawl can certainly be described as a links, although on the higher parts of the course there is a downland-come-heathland flavour. Here is where gorse and broom run amok. For three holes the layout resembles Turnberry as it hugs the shore before turning inland at the 4th. The finest hole may be the 9th, a shortish, sweeping dog-leg that features a downhill drive and a tricky uphill approach to a green which slopes from back to front and is surrounded by pot bunkers. However the most exciting and exhilarating hole is saved until last. The 18th charges downhill to a green perched right on the edge of the ocean. Enjoy Porthcawl... but beware the smiler with the knife.

COURSE INFORMATION & FACILITIES

Royal Porthcawl Golf Club
Rest Bay, Porthcawl
Mid Glamorgan CF36 3UW.

Secretary: Frank Prescott.
Tel: 01656 782251. Fax: 01656 771687.
Golf Professional Peter Evans Tel: 01656 773702.

Green Fees per 18 holes per day:
Weekdays – £40. Weekends – £50.
Weekdays (day) – £50. Weekends (day) – £60.
Letter of introduction and handicap certificate required.
Some time restrictions.

CARD OF THE COURSE – PAR 72

1	2	3	4	5	6	7	8	9	Out
326	429	388	193	483	384	120	454	379	3156
Par 4	Par 4	Par 4	Par 3	Par 5	Par 4	Par 3	Par 5	Par 4	Par 36

10	11	12	13	14	15	16	17	18	In
327	183	437	425	148	421	420	506	383	3250
Par 4	Par 3	Par 5	Par 4	Par 3	Par 4	Par 4	Par 5	Par 4	Par 36

HOW TO GET THERE

ave the M4 motorway at
nction 37, (ignore all signs
Porthcawl shown before
nction 37). Follow the signs to
rthcawl (3 miles), at the large
undabout at the entrance to
rthcawl take a right turn off
e roundabout
d follow
ns to
st Bay
RPGC.

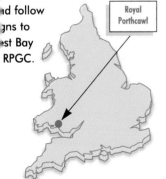

Royal
Porthcawl

Royal St. David's

With a St Andrews in Scotland and a St George's in England, it seems only right that there should be a St David's in Wales. Along with Royal Porthcawl in the South, the Royal St David's Golf Club at Harlech is one of the principality's two greatest Championship links.

Of its many attributes, St David's is perhaps best known for its glorious setting: on the one side stretch the blue waters of Tremedog Bay, and on the other, the imperious Snowdon and the other great mountains of Snowdonia National Park; while surveying all from its lofty perch is the almost forbidding presence of Harlech Castle. The massive fortress built by Edward I has known a particularly turbulent past. It played a

prominent role in the War of the Roses when a great siege took place eventually ending in surrender. The siege is commemorated in the famous song 'Men of Harlech'.

Measuring less than 6500 yards from the championship tees, St David's may not at first glance seem overly testing. However, the general consensus is that the course 'plays long'. Par is a very tight 69 and there are only two par fives on the card. Furthermore the rough can be very punishing and it is rare for there not to be a stiff westerly wind. Perhaps the most difficult holes on the course are the 10th, a long par four that is usually played into the prevailing wind, and the classic 15th which requires a lengthy, angled drive followed by a precise approach.

COURSE INFORMATION & FACILITIES

Royal St David's Golf Club
Harlech
Gwynedd LL46 2UB.

Secretary: David Morkill
Tel: 01766 780361.
Fax: 01766 781110.

Golf Professional John Barnet Tel: 01766 780857.

Green Fees per 18 holes per day:
Weekdays – £35.   Weekends – £40.
Weekdays (day) – £35.   Weekends (day) – £40.
Handicap certificate required. Some tine restrictions.

CARD OF THE COURSE (Championship) – PAR 69

1	2	3	4	5	6	7	8	9	Out
436	373	463	188	393	401	494	513	173	3434
Par 4	Par 4	Par 4	Par 3	Par 4	Par 4	Par 5	Par 5	Par 3	Par 36

10	11	12	13	14	15	16	17	18	In
458	144	437	451	218	427	354	427	202	3118
Par 4	Par 3	Par 4	Par 4	Par 3	Par 4	Par 4	Par 4	Par 3	Par 33

HOW TO GET THERE

ourse is located on A496 at
ower Harlech.

Royal St. David's
Golf Club

Royal St. George's

I t is difficult to say which is the more distinguished – the golf club or the golf course. Royal St George's was the first English club to host the Open Championship. This was in 1894, just seven years after the club's formation. Today, more than a century later, the links is one of only three English venues still on the championship rota – in 2003 the Open will be played here for a 13th time.

Whether you prefer Royal St George's or Royal Birkdale – they are generally considered to be the country's two finest links courses – will largely depend on whether you believe links golf holes are better, or more enjoyable to play, if they find a route in between or alongside their accompanying sand dunes (preferably with fairways running through valleys where the lies are relatively level), or whether you favour links holes that career headlong into the dunes (occasionally clambering over the top of them, resulting in the odd blind shot and awkward stance). If you are in the latter camp you will cast your vote for Royal St George's.

It is a classic links. Laid out amid a vast area of rugged duneland, each hole at St George's appears to occupy a world of its own; the challenge is formidable and yet there is an immense sense of freedom. The golf course exudes a spirit of adventure.

There is not a weak hole at St George's, but among the most celebrated are the 4th, a heroic par four that features 'the tallest and deepest bunker in the United Kingdom', and the short 6th, the fabled 'Maiden'.

COURSE INFORMATION & FACILITIES

Royal St. George's
Sandwich
Kent. CT13 9PB

Secretary: Gerald E Watts.
Tel: 01304 613090. Fax: 01304 611245.

Golf Professional Andrew Brooks Tel: 01304 615236.

Green Fees:
Weekdays – £65. Weekdays (day) – £90.
Letter of introduction and Handicap certificate required.
Some time restrictions.

CARD OF THE COURSE – PAR 70

1	2	3	4	5	6	7	8	9	Out
441	376	210	468	421	155	530	418	389	3408
Par 4	Par 4	Par 3	Par 4	Par 4	Par 3	Par 5	Par 4	Par 4	Par 35

10	11	12	13	14	15	16	17	18	In
413	216	365	443	551	478	163	425	468	3522
Par 4	Par 3	Par 4	Par 4	Par 5	Par 4	Par 3	Par 4	Par 4	Par 35

HOW TO GET THERE

rom M2 take A2 to
Canterbury; then A257 to
andwich. From M20 (Dover)
ike A256 to Sandwich.
oyal St George's is situated
n minor road to Sandwich
ay.

Royal
St. George's

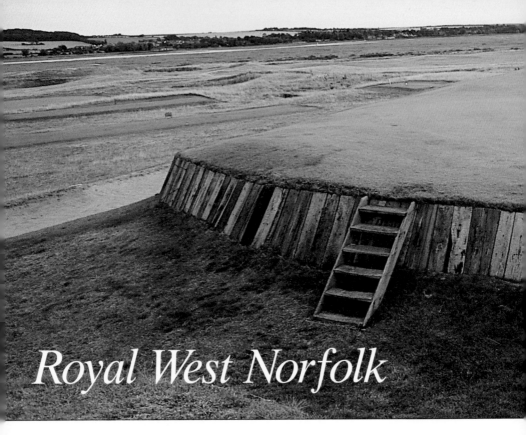

Royal West Norfolk

The Royal West Norfolk Golf Club at Brancaster exudes a unique sense of tradition, history and character. This testing and most enjoyable links lies in a range of sand hills between marshland and sea. The road that leads to the course can flood at very high tide; at such times a discerning golfer may choose to leave his car in the village and walk the remainder of the journey!

Laid out in 1891, the Prince of Wales immediately bestowed patronage on the club. The Royal flavour has prevailed and there have been no fewer than four Royal Captains, most recently the Duke of Kent in 1981. The links has remained refreshingly unaltered over the years, although two greens were lost to the sea in 1939 and 1940.

A traditional out and back links layout, the character of Brancaster is exemplified by both the tidal marshes (which come into play around the 8th and 9th) and the famed wooden sleepered bunkers, many of which are cross bunkers and which are introduced as early as the 3rd. Although the shorter of the two nines, the inward half is often the more testing as it is invariably played into a stiff westerly wind. The 11th and 12th are located deep amid the dunes but the famous old 14th, where the fairway tumbles along classic linksland close to the shore, is perhaps the most difficult hole of all. After a strong finish, with sleepered bunkers both to the front and back of the 18th green, the homely nineteenth hole provides a final treat.

HOW TO GET THERE

miles east of Hunstanton.
Brancaster Village, turn
orth at Beach/Broad Lane
unction with A149. Club is
mile down this road.

Royal West
Norfolk

COURSE INFORMATION & FACILITIES

Royal West Norfolk Golf Club
Brancaster, Near King's Lynn
Norfolk PE31 8AX.

Secretary: Major N. A. Carrington Smith.
Tel: 01485 210087. Fax: 01485 210087.

Golf Professional S.Rayner Tel: 01485 210616.

Green Fees per 18 holes per day:
Weekdays (Summer) – £43. Weekends (Summer) - £60.
Weekdays (Winter) – £40. Weekends (Winter) - £45.
Handicap certificate required. Some time restrictions.

CARD OF THE COURSE – PAR 71

1	2	3	4	5	6	7	8	9	Out
413	442	401	122	4151	182	481	492	403	3351
Par 4	Par 4	Par 4	Par 3	Par 4	Par 3	Par 5	Par 5	Par 4	Par 36

10	11	12	13	14	15	16	17	18	In
147	474	377	304	428	186	335	390	379	3020
Par 3	Par 5	Par 4	Par 4	Par 4	Par 3	Par 4	Par 4	Par 4	Par 35

Saunton

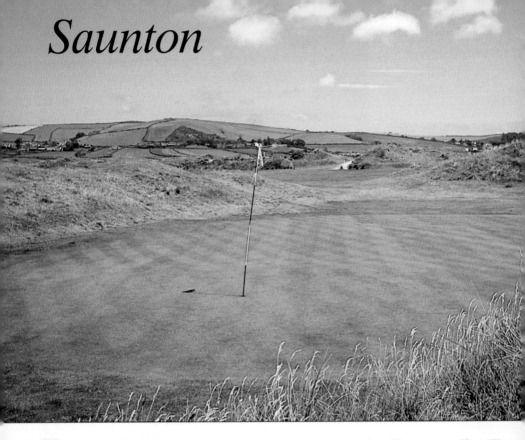

*I*f the Open Championship is ever
taken to the south west of England
the two most likely venues are
Burnham and Berrow in Somerset and
Saunton in north Devon. Both regularly
host major amateur events and both
would test the world's best with a classic
examination of links golf. If the setting
were the determining factor, Saunton
would have the edge. Separated from
one of Britain's finest beaches by a vast
range of sand hills, Saunton has a rugged
beauty. It also has 36 holes to savour
with the championship East Course and
the newer, slightly shorter West Course.

While not as ancient as nearby
Westward Ho!, Saunton celebrated its
centenary in 1997. At first there were just
nine holes and the clubhouse was a single

room next to the village post office. The
course was extended to 18 holes before
the First World War but it wasn't until
the 1930s that Saunton's reputation
was really established. Most responsible
was golf architect Herbert Fowler.
The creator of Walton Heath, Fowler
designed the East Course. Although some
alterations were made in the 1950s, it
remains his greatest seaside achievement.

The East begins with four strong
holes, each measuring over 400 yards.
The 5th is an excellent par three but
perhaps the best two holes are the long
14th, with its elevated tee and ever-
narrowing fairway, and the 16th, a superb
par four featuring a drive over a large
sandhill and an approach that must carry
a deep bunker to find a bowl-shaped green

DEVON

CARD OF THE COURSE (East) – PAR 71

1	2	3	4	5	6	7	8	9	Out
478	476	402	441	122	370	428	380	392	3489
Par 4	Par 5	Par 4	Par 4	Par 3	Par 4	Par 4	Par 4	Par 4	Par 36

10	11	12	13	14	15	16	17	18	In
337	362	414	145	455	478	434	207	408	3240
Par 4	Par 4	Par 4	Par 3	Par 4	Par 5	Par 4	Par 3	Par 4	Par 35

HOW TO GET THERE

From the M5, leave at Junction 27 and follow the A361 to Barnstaple. In Barnstaple follow the A361 to Braunton and at Braunton turn left at the main traffic lights towards Saunton and Croyde. The Golf Club is about 2 miles out of Braunton on the left.

Saunton
Golf Club

Seacroft

*I*t is hard to believe that south east Lincolnshire was once one of the most populated areas of Great Britain. Apparently the region was buzzing in the late Middle Ages, but nowadays it has been left largely to the birds - literally so, just five miles south of Skegness at a wildlife sanctuary called (rather interestingly) Gibraltar Point. And midway between Skegness and Gibraltar Point there is a hidden, almost secret golf course named Seacroft. In actual fact, Seacroft is the finest links course on the east coast of England between Hunstanton and Seaton Carew.

Overlooking The Wash, Seacroft is a decidedly old fashioned links; its layout, crafted initially by Tom Dunn in 1892, and later revised by Sir Guy Campbell, stretches out and back à la St Andrews. The two nines occupy distinct levels with a central ridge of dunes dividing one half from the other.

The terrain is similar to that of Hunstanton and the quality of the golf is only slightly inferior. The par threes holes are particularly memorable - all four are even-numbered (something to remember when playing foursomes!) while the par fours provide plenty of variey but rarely much margin for error. As Donald Steel has observed, 'On nearly every tee, it is a case of looking down a gun barrel'. The best of the two-shot holes is probably the 13th, a reachable par five, and which in terms of character and quality is reminiscent of the much acclaimed 13th hole at Silloth-on-Solway.

COURSE INFORMATION & FACILITIES

Seacroft Golf Club
Drummond Road, Skegness,
Lincolnshire PE25 3AU

Secretary/Director: Richard England
Tel: 01754 763020.

Golf Professional Robin Lawie Tel: 01754 769624.

Green Fees:
Weekdays – £25. Weekends – £30.
Weekdays (days) £35. Weekends (day) £40.
Handicap certificate required.

CARD OF THE COURSE – PAR 71

1	2	3	4	5	6	7	8	9	Out
409	369	328	184	439	343	422	390	484	3368
Par 4	Par 4	Par 4	Par 3	Par 4	Par 4	Par 4	Par 4	Par 5	Par 36

10	11	12	13	14	15	16	17	18	In
153	538	210	499	175	400	313	414	409	3111
Par 3	Par 5	Par 3	Par 5	Par 3	Par 4	Par 4	Par 4	Par 4	Par 35

HOW TO GET THERE

ollow the signs to the Seafront
the "Clock Tower", 20 yards
om the "Clock Tower" turn
ght onto Drumond Road, drive
long approximately 1 mile. 100
ards past the "Crown Hotel" on
ae left, The Clubhouse (a white
uilding & the first tee are
here). Any signs for
Gibraltar Point"
ill take you
ast the
ourse.

Seacroft
Golf Club

THE
VINE HOTEL
SEACROFT
SKEGNESS
PE25 3DB

Located only 300 yds from Seacroft Golf Course, Skegness' premier hotel offers
superb accommodation, fine wines, excellent food and Batemans award winning ales.
Set amidst tranquil gardens. The Vine is the ideal place to relax after the game.
Small golf parties or societies are welcome at specially discounted rates.

Telephone: 01754 610611 Fax: 01754 769845
Web Site: http://www.skegness-resort.co.uk/vine

59

Seaton Carew

Seaton Carew near Hartlepool is a place of extraordinary contrasts. Here is where the industrial north east collides head on with a popular seaside resort. The North Sea washes a sweep of golden sand; beyond this beach are the dunes; beyond the dunes is the lively town (where in summer sedate guesthouses jostle for prominence with noisy arcades) and beyond the town is a backdrop of towering chimneys and their modern equivalents, which at night appear lit up like giant torches. Oh, we forgot to mention one thing: on the landward side of the dunes – though occasionally wandering in amongst them – is the Seaton Carew championship golf links. Same as and right next to Seacroft!

The two outstanding sequences at Seaton Carew occur around the turn and over the closing stretch, where sand dunes, undulating terrain, traditional seaside bunkers and a mass of buckthorn conspire to provide an exacting but enjoyable finish.

The par four 9th, 'Lagoon' is possibly the best hole on the front nine. The lagoon itself – essentially marshy ground – lies to the right of the fairway yet a tee shot directed to this side sets up a much easier second to a green with a steep fall-away on the right.

The 17th at Seaton Carew features a bold drive over dunes and gorse and an approach to a raised green surrounded by subtle contours. The 18th has plenty of character too, with an out of bounds to the right and a rippling fairway.

COURSE INFORMATION & FACILITIES

Seaton Carew Golf Club
Tees Road,
Hartlepool. TS25 1DE

Secretary: Peter R Wilson
Tel: 01429 261473.

Golf Professional Bill Hector Tel: 01429 890660.

Green Fees:
Weekdays – £25. Weekends – £33.
Weekdays (day) – £29. Weekends (day) – £40.
Handicap certificate required. Some time restrictions.

CARD OF THE COURSE – PAR 73

1	2	3	4	5	6	7	8	9	Out
358	560	168	385	373	165	354	355	371	3089
Par 4	Par 5	Par 3	Par 4	Par 4	Par 3	Par 4	Par 4	Par 4	Par 35
10	11	12	13	14	15	16	17	18	In
390	471	386	559	525	203	445	397	392	3768
Par 4	Par 5	Par 4	Par 5	Par 5	Par 3	Par 4	Par 4	Par 4	Par 38

HOW TO GET THERE

9 North. A689 Hartlepool, follow signs
Seaton Carew at south end of village on
t hand side.

Seaton Carew
Golf Club

the Staincliffe
H O T E L

The Cliff,

Seaton Carew,

Hartlepool. TS25 1AB

Tel: 01429 264301

Fax:01429 421366

The Staincliffe Hotel is a picturesque pre-victorian Hotel situated on the coast with superb views of the sea, recently re-developed to the highest standards under the supervision of Redhouse Design in Newcastle, with interiors designed by Helen Morris at the award winning Stencil Library. Renowned for its warm hospitality and welcoming staff, the rooms and themed suites surpass the highest expectations while still remaining affordably priced. A superb wine cellar complements an extensive and varied á la carte menu blending classical dishes with traditional British cuisine.

Silloth on Solway

*C*ecil Leitch, one of Britain's finest ever lady golfers, once said: 'If you can play Silloth you can play anywhere'. The four times British Ladies champion should have been able to judge better than most for she grew up in Silloth and it was here that she and her four golfing sisters learned to play.

Silloth is a magnificent links and yet, despite its having staged several major championships, it remains one of Britain's lesser known (and most underrated) golfing gems. The sole reason is, of course, its remoteness, but a journey to Silloth will never disappoint, since not only does the course provide a wonderful golfing experience but the Silloth Club is one of the friendliest and most welcoming in Britain.

A cursory glance at the score card is unlikely to instil fear into the heart of the first time visitor, although anyone who has stood on the 1st tee with the wind hammering into their face will attest to how demanding a challenge this can be. The course meanders its way through and over some classic links terrain. There are occasional spectacular vantage points – the coastal views from the 4th and 6th tees being especially memorable – and the round calls for many courageous strokes. The greatest hole is the par five 13th, 'Hog's Back', which features an exceptionally narrow fairway and a severely plateaued green. If you hit a good drive it is difficult to resist going for the green in two – a failed attempt, however, spells disaster!

HOW TO GET THERE

om the South: M6 Junction
I onto B5305 to Wigton,
en B5302 to Silloth.
om North East: M6
nction 43 take A69
arlisle A595/596 to Wigton
en B5302 toSilloth.

Silloth
Golf Club

COURSE INFORMATION & FACILITIES

Silloth on Solway Golf Club
The Clubhouse, Silloth
Carlisle, Cumbria CA5 4BL

Secretary: John G. Proudlock.
Tel: 016973 31782.

Golf Professional Alan Mackenzie Tel: 016973 31782.

Green Fees per 18 holes per day:
Weekdays (day) – £25. Weekends (round) – £32.
Letter of introduction and handicap certificate required.
Some time restrictions.

CARD OF THE COURSE – PAR 72

1	2	3	4	5	6	7	8	9	Out
380	320	371	372	518	201	424	371	134	3091
Par 4	Par 4	Par 4	Par 4	Par 5	Par 3	Par 4	Par 4	Par 3	Par 35

10	11	12	13	14	15	16	17	18	In
318	403	204	511	512	444	200	495	438	3525
Par 4	Par 4	Par 3	Par 5	Par 5	Par 4	Par 3	Par 5	Par 4	Par 37

St. Enodoc

Situated on the sometimes rugged, sometimes romantic coast of north Cornwall, St Enodoc is a classic and staunchly old fashioned links course: here is a land of huge sand hills, of tumbling fairways, hidden pot bunkers, awkward stances, the occasional blind shot and firm, fast greens. An exhilarating links, although not long at just over 6200 yards, it is exacting in its demand for skill and judgement and memorable for its special features.

Since 1982 there have been two 18 hole courses at St Enodoc. The main course is now named the Church Course, and the newer, shorter layout is called the Holywell Course. The main links takes its name from the little half-sunken church which is located near the far end of the course. This church threatens to come into play at the par four 10th, the most difficult hole on the course.

The drive at the 10th is dramatically downhill and it must carry almost 200 yards to find a narrow, heavily contoured fairway; off to the left is a marshy area and a stream, while to the right are steep dunes and uncompromising rough. The approach to the green is almost as daunting as the tee shot!

The other hole at St Enodoc that everyone talks about is the 6th, there players must confront the 'Himalayas', 'the highest sandhill, to the best of my belief, I have ever seen on a golf course', remarked the famous golf writer, Bernard Darwin. With holes like the 6th, it isn't hard to see why St Endoc is so often likened to Prestwick.

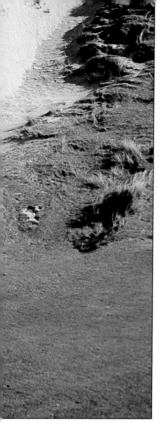

CARD OF THE COURSE – PAR 69

1	2	3	4	5	6	7	8	9	Out
518	438	436	292	161	378	394	155	393	3165
Par 5	Par 4	Par 4	Par 4	Par 3	Par 4	Par 4	Par 3	Par 4	Par 35

10	11	12	13	14	15	16	17	18	In
457	205	386	360	355	168	495	206	446	3078
Par 4	Par 3	Par 4	Par 4	Par 4	Par 3	Par 5	Par 3	Par 4	Par 34

HOW TO GET THERE

om Wadebridge follow
e signs to Rock. Go right
rough Rock until you see a
ɡn for St Enodoc Golf Club
 the right hand side.

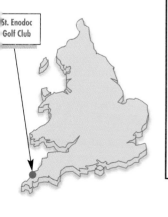

St. Enodoc
Golf Club

Tenby

As any toddler will tell you, some of the finest beaches in the British Isles are to be found in the south and west of Wales, and two of the finest sandy stretches in this region are to be found at the beautiful resort of Tenby in Pembrokeshire: Tenby North Beach and Tenby South Beach. Both provide magnificent views of monastic Caldey Island, while amid the dunes overlooking the glorious sweep of South Beach is the classic links of Tenby Golf Club.

Tenby lays claim to being the oldest constituted club in the Principality, having been founded in 1888. Although it has staged many important events, nowadays the links is regarded as a little too short and, like Pennard, a little too 'quaint and quirky' to host important championships.

More is the pity, for Tenby is a 19th century masterpiece – wonderfully old fashioned (and proud of it). The fairways twist and tumble with utter irregularity; the course's unpredictability is its charm and strength.

Two of the most interesting holes are the 3rd ('Dai Rees') and the 4th ('Bell'). The former features a hog's back fairway and a narrow table-shaped green guarded by deep pot bunkers. The 4th is played from an elevated tee along an undulating fairway bordered by huge dunes; the approach is blind, down to a green concealed in a dell. On the back nine the 12th is an excellent par three and the closing hole, a par four known as 'Charlie's Whiskers', bristles with character.

HOW TO GET THERE

4 to Carmarthen.
ead for St. Clears,
getty and then Tenby.

Tenby
Golf Club

COURSE INFORMATION & FACILITIES

Tenby Golf Club
The Burrows, Tenby
Pembrokeshire SA70 7NP.

Secretary: J. A. Pearson.
Tel: 01834 842978.

Golf Professional: Mark Hawkey Tel: 01834 844447.

Green Fees:
Weekdays – £25. Weekends – £30.
Weekdays (day) – £25. Weekends (day) – £30.

Handicap certificate required. Some time restrictions.

CARD OF THE COURSE – PAR 69

1	2	3	4	5	6	7	8	9	Out
466	424	380	417	353	121	414	365	185	3125
Par 4	Par 4	Par 4	Par 4	Par 4	Par 3	Par 4	Par 4	Par 3	Par 34

10	11	12	13	14	15	16	17	18	In
422	410	197	287	481	371	384	172	375	3099
Par 4	Par 4	Par 3	Par 4	Par 5	Par 4	Par 4	Par 3	Par 4	Par 35

Wallasey

The links at Wallasey is located on the tip of Cheshire's Wirral Peninsula; the clubhouse overlooks the mouth of the River Mersey. For golf enthusiasts the spectacular North West starts here. Given its geography, it is perhaps not surprising that the course has suffered over the years from coastal erosion. But Wallasey remains an extraordinary site. Some of the sand hills are as impressive as any to be found further north – including those at Birkdale and Hillside – and the layout of the course hurls the golfer headlong into these dunes as early as the 2nd hole. With its many elevated tees and plateau greens, the thrill factor is high at Wallasey.

Wallasey is famous as the golfing home of Dr Frank Stableford, the man who invented the Stableford points scoring system. The par three 9th hole is named after him (...four points, then, for a hole-in-one).

Unfortunately the 9th is not one of the strongest holes at Wallasey. The sequence between the 2nd and 5th is probably the best, and certainly most dramatic of the round – the view from the tee at the par five 4th is one not to be rushed – but another good run of holes comes between the 10th and 12th as the course turns back on itself and plunges once more into the dunes. The three hole finish is quite formidable, comprising a huge par three (with its elegant, shelf-like green guarded by a vast dune, the 16th may be the finest hole of all) and two crunchingly long par fours.

COURSE INFORMATION & FACILITIES

Wallasey Golf Club
Baywater Road, Wallasey
Wirral L45 8LA.

Secretary: Mrs. L.M.Dolman.
Tel: 0151 691 1024. Fax: 0151 638 8988.

Golf Professional Mike Adams Tel: 0151 638 3888.

Green Fees:
Weekdays (round) – £39, Weekends (round) – £42.
Weekdays (day) – £42, Weekends (day) – £48.
Letter of introduction and handicap certificate required.
Some time restrictions.

CARD OF THE COURSE – PAR 72

1	2	3	4	5	6	7	8	9	Out
370	443	365	486	165	338	512	385	142	3206
Par 4	Par 4	Par 4	Par 5	Par 3	Par 4	Par 5	Par 4	Par 3	Par 36

10	11	12	13	14	15	16	17	18	In
298	340	137	476	478	358	200	453	398	3138
Par 4	Par 4	Par 3	Par 5	Par 5	Par 4	Par 3	Par 4	Par 4	Par 36

HOW TO GET THERE

om M53 leave Junction 1.
llow A554, signs for New
ighton. On leaving the
ur road and joining
yswater Road the
ubhouse is situated
proximately a quarter
a mile down
e road on
e left
nd
le.

Wallasey
Golf Club

West Cornwall

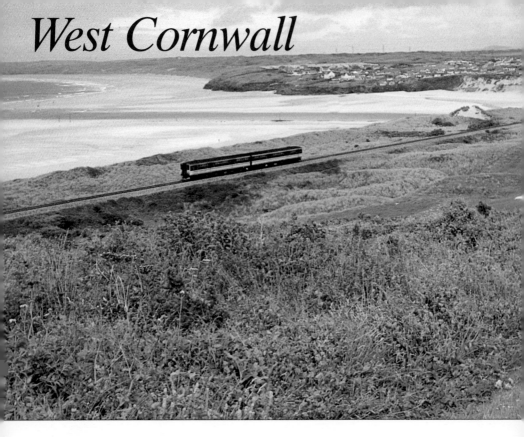

Certain clubs and courses will always be linked with famous players: Walton Heath with James Braid, Hawkstone Park with Sandy Lyle and Ashridge with Henry Cotton. So it is with the delightful West Cornwall links situated at Lelant, a tiny village near St Ives. Jim Barnes, winner of the Open Championship on both sides of the Atlantic during the 1920s was born in Lelant in 1887. 'Long Jim', as he was known (he was as tall as Nick Faldo) learned his golf at West Cornwall before emigrating to America when he was 19.

Notwithstanding the fact that St Ives is a celebrated beauty spot, a favourite haunt of fishermen and artists, the links is undeniably remote. And yet it has immense charm: the scenery is breathtaking and the course itself bristles with character. It is quite short by modern standards - having changed little since Long Jim's day. The terrain is perfect for links golf and the greens are invariably firm and fast. Moreover, the sand hills at Lelant are not merely ornamental for, in a manner akin to Tenby in South Wales, the course careers headlong into the dunes.

The challenge begins with an extremely long par three at which the tee shot must be aimed at the spire of St Uny Church. The 2nd is a superb two-shotter, but perhaps the most memorable holes are those between the 5th and 8th where the course runs very close to the sea. The most spectacular views can be enjoyed from the 12th tee.

HOW TO GET THERE

30 past Truro towards
Penzance. Turn off Hayle by-
pass towards St. Ives. Enter
Lelant village, turn 1st right
past 'The Badger Inn' and
follow signt to West
Cornwall Golf Club. Approx
¼ mile from
30.

West Cornwall
Golf Club

COURSE INFORMATION & FACILITIES

West Cornwall Golf Club
Church Lane, Lelant, St. Ives,
Cornwall TR26 3DZ.

Secretary: Malcolm Lack.
Tel/Fax: 01736 753401.

Golf Professional: Paul Atherton Tel: 01736 753177.
Fax: 01736 75340

Green Fees: Weekdays – £20. Weekends – £25.
Weekdays (day) – £20. Weekends (day) – £25.

Handicap certificate required.

CARD OF THE COURSE – PAR 69

1	2	3	4	5	6	7	8	9	Out
229	382	342	352	179	337	191	325	406	2743
Par 3	Par 4	Par 4	Par 4	Par 3	Par 4	Par 3	Par 4	Par 4	Par 33

10	11	12	13	14	15	16	17	18	In
331	362	494	264	446	135	521	194	394	3141
Par 4	Par 4	Par 5	Par 4	Par 4	Par 3	Par 5	Par 3	Par 4	Par 36

Kilchurn Castle, Loch Awe

Scotland

*S*ince every golfer must play the Old Course at St Andrews at least once in his lifetime, every golfer not living in Scotland must plan at least one golfing trip to the country where it all began. The toughest part is selecting which places to explore in addition to St Andrews.

As this book confines itself to good golf courses situated on the coast – and only true links courses at that – you might reckon that this would narrow down the field considerably. Unfortunately it doesn't. With the exception of the western and north western fringes of Scotland, good links courses are to be found all around the coast. Actually you could plan a week's golf in Scotland and never venture beyond the 'Kingdom of Fife' where St Andrews is located. Several trips, then, would appear in order!

While the east coast can be viewed as the cradle of golf, it was in the south west of Scotland that the oldest major championship was born. The first (British) Open was staged at Prestwick in Ayrshire in 1860. Although the Morris' and the Parks' playground is still largely intact, it no longer hosts the championship, but neighbouring Troon and Turnberry are both firmly on the Open rota, and since there are several other fine links courses nearby, notably Western Gailes, Ayrshire has considerable appeal.

Further south and further west – almost off the map of Scotland – are two extraordinary links courses: Machrihanish on the Mull of Kintyre and Machrie on the island of Islay. Both are set in stunningly beautiful surroundings and to visit either is to experience golf as it was a century ago. The other outstanding links in the south of Scotland is Southerness on the Solway Firth near Dumfries.

Royal Dornoch is the world's most northerly situated great golf course. It is a classic links – arguably the classic links – and a journey here has become something of a pilgrimage. The road to Dornoch provides an opportunity to inspect Nairn, the venue of the 1999 Walker Cup and another beautiful location. East of Nairn, but still in the north of Scotland, Moray Golf Club at Lossiemouth is well worth a visit and Cruden Bay just south of Peterhead is an absolute must; it is nothing less than the most spectacular links in Scotland.

Heading down the Grampian coast, Aberdeen has two very fine championship links, Royal Aberdeen and Murcar. Of course you could combine a trip to Cruden Bay with a visit to Aberdeen and then, travelling south of the city, pass through Montrose where there is a very underrated links, and arrive in Carnoustie. After the 1999 Open few would challenge Carnoustie's reputation as Scotland's toughest links. But it is more than that: Walter Hagen once declared it to be Britain's greatest links.

The 'Kingdom of Fife' now beckons. Close to St Andrews is Crail, home of the seventh oldest golf club in the world and which now has two links courses to savour with the recent addition of the acclaimed Craighead Links. Lundin's golf course has plenty of character, but the one everyone is talking about is the new links at Kingsbarns; to quote Canadian writer Lorne Rubenstein, "It's difficult to imagine a worthier spiritual descendant of the Old Course."

Last but not least there is the Lothian region. Muirfield may not be the easiest place to arrange a game – although it is possible with advance planning, but Gullane, North Berwick and Dunbar welcome visitors with open arms – moreover, they provide a perfect introduction to links golf in Scotland.

CARNOUSTIE	NAIRN
CRAIL	NORTH BERWICK
CRUDEN BAY	PRESTWICK
DUNBAR	ROYAL ABERDEEN
GULLANE	ROYAL DORNOCH
KINGSBARNS	ROYAL TROON
LUNDIN	SOUTHERNESS
MACHRIHANISH	ST ANDREWS OLD COURSE
MONTROSE	THE MACHRIE
MORAY	TURNBERRY
MURCAR	WESTERN GAILES

Scotland

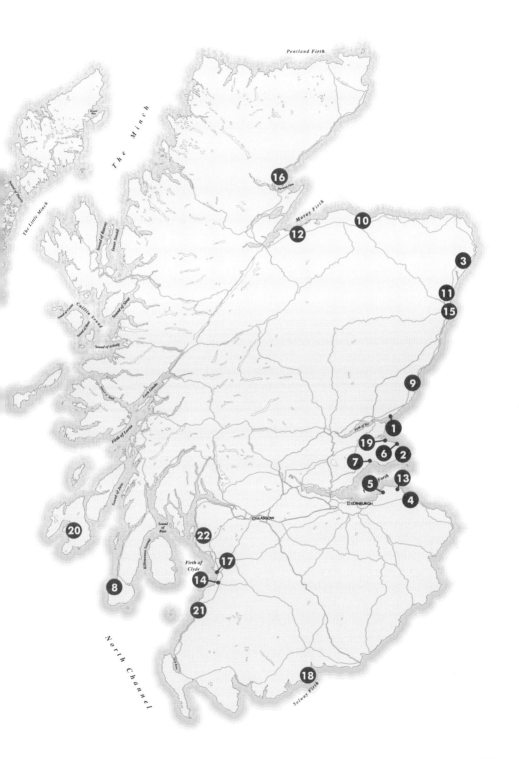

Carnoustie

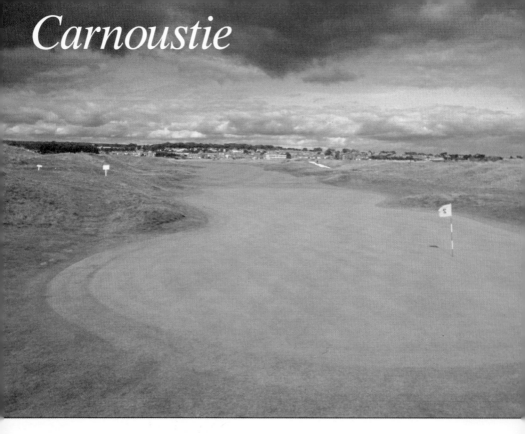

*O*nce described as a 'great big shaggy monster', Carnoustie is acknowledged to be the toughest golf course on the Open Championship rota. Indeed, only Royal County Down in Northern Ireland can seriously dispute its claim to being the most demanding links course on the planet.

What makes Carnoustie so difficult? Its length for a start. For the 1999 Open, Carnoustie weighed in at a prodigious 7,361 yards, par 71. When the wind blows several of the par fours are unreachable in two shots – and the notorious par three 16th is likely to require two strokes before the sanctuary of the green is found. The punishing nature of its hazards is the other major reason.

Bunkers and burns. Carnoustie's bunkers are legendary; there are plenty of them, and the majority are very large, very deep and perfectly positioned to trap errant shots. A number of Scottish links courses possess a meandering burn – St Andrews, Prestwick and Turnberry immediately spring to mind, but how many have two? Carnoustie has the Barry Burn and Jockie's Burn, and they have a habit of traversing the fairways in the most unfriendly of places.

Perhaps more than anything, though, Carnoustie's fearsome reputation centres on its incredibly difficult finishing stretch. From the 15th tee to the 18th green, Carnoustie bears its teeth like no other links.

COURSE INFORMATION & FACILITIES

Carnoustie Golf Links
Links Parade, Carnoustie, Angus. DD7 7JE

Secretary: John Martin
Tel: 01241 853789   Fax: 01241 852720

Golf Professional: Lee Vannet
Tel: 01241 853789   Fax: 01241 852050

Green Fees:
Weekdays - £70, Weekends - £70,
Weekdays (day) - £70, Weekends (day) - £70
Handicap certificate required. Time restrictions apply.

CARD OF THE COURSE (Championship) – PAR 72

1	2	3	4	5	6	7	8	9	Out
401	435	337	375	387	520	394	167	413	3429
Par 4	Par 4	Par 4	Par 4	Par 4	Par 5	Par 4	Par 3	Par 4	Par 36

10	11	12	13	14	15	16	17	18	In
446	362	479	161	483	459	245	433	444	3512
Par 4	Par 4	Par 5	Par 3	Par 5	Par 4	Par 3	Par 4	Par 4	Par 36

HOW TO GET THERE

ourse is situated at
arnoustie, north east
om Dundee.

Carnoustie
Golf Links

Crail

*O*n 23rd February 1786 eleven gentlemen assembled at the Golf Inn in Crail and together formed the Crail Golfing Society. The records of that historic day are still preserved; indeed, the seventh oldest golf club in the world possesses a complete set of minutes from the date of its inception.

The records reveal that the original members took their golf seriously. Their golfing attire included scarlet jackets with yellow buttons and after a day on the links they would adjourn to the Golf Inn for 'happy evenings with accustomed hilarity and good fellowship.'

The Crail Golfing Society initially played on a narrow strip of land at Sauchope, before moving to Fifeness and the Balcomie Links in 1895. Having now

entered its third century, it clearly remains a progressive club for it has recently constructed a second 18 hole course, the Craighead Links, which was designed by one of America's most talented and traditionally oriented golf architects, Gil Hanse.

With 36 holes to savour, Crail has become a 'must visit' venue for golfers exploring the kingdom of Fife. None are likely to be disappointed. The Balcomie Links remains one of Scotland's most sporting and attractive links with views of the sea from every hole. The Craighead Links is a little longer and more challenging. It too is beautifully situated and, best of all, it looks and plays like a century old links.

HOW TO GET THERE

om Edinburgh follow A92
Kirkaldy, then the A915
Leven. Take B942 to
tenweem. Follow
e A917 to Crail.
om Dundee take
?1 onto St Andrews,
en the A917 to Crail

Crail
Golf Club

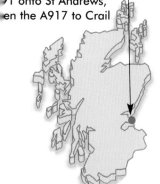

COURSE INFORMATION & FACILITIES

 Crail Golfing Society
Balcomie Clubhouse, Fifeness
Crail, Fife KY10 3XN.

Manager: Jim Horsfield.
Tel: 01333 451414. Fax: 01333 450416.

Golf Professional Graeme Lennie Tel: 01333 450960.

Green Fees:
Weekdays – £25. Weekends – £30.
Weekdays (day) – £35. Weekends (day) – £45.
Some time restrictions.

CARD OF THE COURSE – PAR 69

1	2	3	4	5	6	7	8	9	Out
328	494	184	346	459	186	349	442	306	3094
Par 4	Par 5	Par 3	Par 4	Par 4	Par 3	Par 4	Par 4	Par 4	Par 35

10	11	12	13	14	15	16	17	18	In
336	496	528	219	150	270	163	463	203	2828
Par 4	Par 5	Par 5	Par 3	Par 3	Par 4	Par 3	Par 4	Par 3	Par 34

Cruden Bay

*C*ruden Bay is the Ballybunion of Scotland. Really? OK, so it's nowhere near as famous as the great Irish links, and the club does not boast 36 holes, but in terms of character, visual appeal and an ability to set golfers' pulses racing, Cruden Bay is Scotland's nearest equivalent. Oh, and I nearly forgot, Tom Watson raves about the place.

A few years back the five times British Open Champion, whose regular visit to Ballybunion in the 1980s ensured that club's worldwide popularity, dropped in on Cruden Bay practically unannounced. The second he set eyes on the links he would have been mesmerised, for the view from the elevated clubhouse rivals any in the golfing world. The sand dunes at Cruden Bay are vast and impressive; beyond the dunes is a stunning beach.

The golf course tumbles in and out of the dunes and, for several holes, runs right alongside the beach. It is thrilling, cavalier golf, and immensely entertaining.

If there is a criticism of Cruden Bay then it might be said that it is a little quirky, that there are a few too many blind shots. Perhaps in this regard, the links more closely resembles Lahinch. Also, the 1st, 17th and 18th holes are similar to several at Royal Dornoch, with rippling fairways, plateau greens and rampant gorse. A confused identity, or an embarrassment of riches?

Located 23 miles north of Aberdeen and 7 miles south of Peterhead, Cruden Bay is not the most accessible of links courses. But it offers one of the world's truly great golfing experiences.

COURSE INFORMATION & FACILITIES

Cruden Bay Golf Club
Aulton Road, Cruden Bay
Peterhead AB42 0NN.

Secretary/Manager:
Mrs. Rosemary Pittendrigh.
Tel: 01779 812285. Fax: 01779 812945.

Golf Professional: Robbie Stewart
Tel: 01779 812414. Fax: 01779 812414.

Green Fees:
Weekdays – £40. Weekends – £50.
Weekdays (day) – £60.
Handicap certificate required. Some time restrictions.

CARD OF THE COURSE - PAR 70

1	2	3	4	5	6	7	8	9	Out
416	339	286	193	454	529	392	258	462	3329
Par 4	Par 4	Par 4	Par 3	Par 4	Par 5	Par 4	Par 4	Par 4	Par 36

10	11	12	13	14	15	16	17	18	In
385	149	320	550	397	239	182	428	416	3066
Par 4	Par 3	Par 4	Par 5	Par 4	Par 3	Par 3	Par 4	Par 4	Par 34

Red House Hotel

A Traditional Scottish welcome awaits you at the Red House Hotel, situated in the tranquil coastal village of Cruden Bay, only thirty minutes drive from Aberdeen airport. Cruden Bay and the Red House is an ideal base for those interested in golf, bird watching, river and sea angling, or a little history, for the haunting ruins of Slains Castle tower over the cliffs of Cruden Bay's rugged beautiful coast. Naturally being so close to the golf course, the Red House in the first choice for those who wish to play on one of the most beautifully maintained links courses in the United Kingdom.

Aulton Road, Cruden Bay, Peterhead. AB42 7NJ
Tel: 01779 812215   Fax: 01779 812320

HOW TO GET THERE

om Aberdeen
ke A90 Peterhead Road to 'Little
ef' at Foveran. Turn right on A975
ough Newburgh. 10 miles to Cruden
y, Golf Club is first on the right.

om Peterhead
ke A90 Aberdeen Road.
n left at sign post for
den Bay Straight
ough the village
 Golf
b is
 the
.

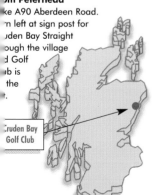

Cruden Bay
Golf Club

Dunbar

*I*t isn't entirely clear when golf was first played at Dunbar. Whilst the Dunbar Golf Club was founded in 1856 following a meeting in the Town Hall, the Dunbar Golfing Society had been instituted in 1794. Furthermore, records indicate that some cruder form of golf had been played in the area early in the 17th century. In 1616 two men of the parish of Tyninghame were censured by the Kirk Session for 'playing at ye nyne holis' on the Lord's Day, and in 1640 an Assistant Minister of Dunbar was disgraced 'for playing at gouff.' Today 'gouff' is still played at Dunbar, although no one is likely to be censured or disgraced for doing so, and there are now 18 splendid holes.

The links is laid out on a fairly narrow tract of land, closely following the contours of the shoreline. It also features (and to an extent is bisected by) an ancient stone wall.

While Dunbar is by no means the longest of Scottish links, when the wind blows it can prove one of the toughest. This may have something to do with the fact that there is an 'Out of Bounds' on the 3rd, 4th, 5th, 6th, 7th, 8th, 9th, 16th, 17th and 18th, and the beach can come into play on no fewer than nine of the holes – straight hitting would appear to be the order of the day!

Dunbar is one of the east coast's most attractive links with some splendid views out across the sea towards Bass Rock. After two fairly gentle par fives and a spectacular par three, the course heads away from the clubhouse along the shore. Some of the finest holes occur around the turn, namely the 9th to the 12th, and the 18th provides a strong finish with the stone wall Out of Bounds running the entire length of the fairway to the right.

COURSE INFORMATION & FACILITIES

Dunbar Golf Club
East Links, Dunbar
East Lothian EH42 1LT.

Secretary: Liz Thom.
Tel: 01368 862317. Fax: 01368 865202.

Golf Professional: Jack Montgomery
Tel: 01368 862086.

Green Fees:
Weekdays – £25. Weekends – £35.
Weekdays (Day) – £35. Weekends (Day) – £45.
Some time restrictions.

CARD OF THE COURSE – PAR 71

1	2	3	4	5	6	7	8	9	Out
474	492	173	353	147	347	382	370	507	3244
Par 5	Par 5	Par 3	Par 4	Par 3	Par 4	Par 4	Par 4	Par 5	Par 37

10	11	12	13	14	15	16	17	18	In
202	418	457	377	432	338	163	338	435	3160
Par 3	Par 4	Par 4	Par 4	Par 4	Par 4	Par 3	Par 4	Par 4	Par 34

HOW TO GET THERE

unbar Golf Club lies to the
ıst of town. From the A1
ɔm Edinburgh take the
1087 into Dunbar. Signs
will direct you to
Club from here.

Dunbar
Golf Club

Marine Hotel

N O R T H   B E R W I C K

The Marine Hotel, a gloriously embellished example of Victoriana, is picturesquely located at the heart of East Lothian's golfing coast. The Marine actually overlooks the 16th hole of North Berwick's championship West Links course which threads along the edge of the Firth of Forth and includes one of golf's most copied holes, the infamous 15th "Redan". Real golf afficionados should take one of the 40 sea view rooms and suites at the rear where they can watch players tackling the West Links course from dusk to dawn.

CROMWELL ROAD NORTH BERWICK. EH39 4LZ
Telephone: 01620 892406 Fax: 01620 894480

Gullane

Stand on the 7th tee on Gullane No. 1 and drink in the view. Then smash your drive downhill! To play golf at Gullane (you must pronounce it 'Gillan') is a sheer delight. There are three courses here: Gullane No 1, Gullane No 2 and, yes, Gullane No 3. All are worthy of a game, but No 1 is most people's favourite.

Like St Andrews and North Berwick, Gullane No 1 starts and finishes in the town. In between it ascends the heights – literally. There is a timeless feel to a round of golf on this ancient links; the mood was perfectly described a century ago by a writer who declared, 'Nowhere else in the world is the golfing prospect so expansive and enticing. Nowhere does the pursuit of the game seem so inevitable.'

Some locals regard Gullane No 1 as the equal of nearby Muirfield. They may be a little biased, although there are certain similarities. In particular, both courses are renowned for the quality of their bunkering. Gullane is not as stern a test of golf and it doesn't possess Muirfield's wealth of architectural subtleties, but then Gullane is less man-made. And besides, Muirfield doesn't have those spectacular 360 degree views.

The 7th is inevitably the most memorable hole on the front nine but the back nine has the greater number of strong holes, notably the 11th, 15th and 16th. Like the 7th, the 17th charges downhill and the 18th guides you back into town.

EAST LOTHIAN

CARD OF THE COURSE – PAR 71

1	2	3	4	5	6	7	8	9	Out
302	379	496	144	450	324	398	332	151	2976
Par 4	Par 4	Par 5	Par 3	Par 4	Par 4	Par 4	Par 4	Par 3	Par 36

10	11	12	13	14	15	16	17	18	In
466	471	480	170	435	537	186	390	355	3512
Par 4	Par 4	Par 5	Par 3	Par 4	Par 5	Par 3	Par 4	Par 4	Par 36

HOW TO GET THERE

8 Miles East of Edinburgh
n A198.

Gullane
Golf Club

Kingsbarns Golf Links

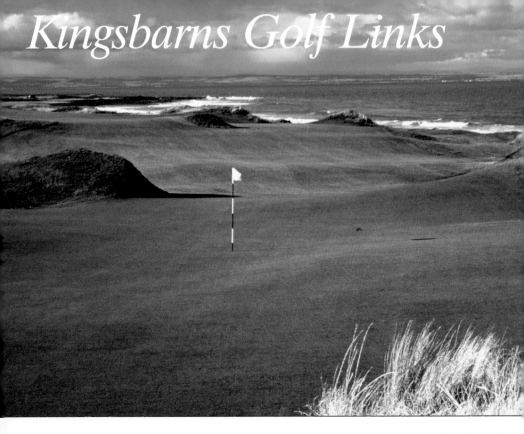

*I*t seems rather appropriate that a golf course hailed as 'one of the last and best links courses ever to be built in the British Isles' should be situated just down the road from the greatest and oldest links of all. Kingsbarns is a mere five miles from St Andrews.

How new and how good is Kingsbarns? It is intended that the course will officially open for play during the week of the 2000 Open Championship at St Andrews - this makes it pretty new; in some ways, however, the golf course is actually quite ancient. Golf was played on the site of the new links at least as long ago as the 18th century, and historical records relate that the Kingsbarns Golf Society played over a nine hole course here from 1815,

making it the 12th oldest golf club in the world. In 1939 golf ceased to be played at Kingsbarns. As the new links has 18 (very different) holes it could hardly be described as a revived Kingsbarns, but we can say that its golfing roots are deep.

New or not-so-new, Kingsbarns is certainly receiving rave reviews. Designed by the American architects Kyle Phillips and Mark Parsinen, seven holes at Kingsbarns run adjacent to the shore while the other eleven offer views of the sea.

It may be too early to judge just how good Kingsbarns is but, if it plays half as good as it looks, Scotland will have another outstanding links to tempt overseas golfing visitors.

COURSE INFORMATION & FACILITIES

Kingsbarns Golf Links
Kingsbarns
Fife, KY16 8QD

Administration Manager:
Donna Clark Tel: 01334 880222.

Director of Golf: David Scott Tel: 01334 880222.

Green Fees:
Weekdays – £85. Weekends – £85.

Restrictions: None
Caddies available on request. Club & shoe hire also available.

CARD OF THE COURSE – PAR 72

1	2	3	4	5	6	7	8	9	Out
425	200	525	420	380	330	470	175	565	3490
Par 4	Par 3	Par 5	Par 4	Par 4	Par 4	Par 4	Par 3	Par 5	Par 36

10	11	12	13	14	15	16	17	18	In
395	435	590	145	365	205	570	470	445	3620
Par 4	Par 4	Par 5	Par 3	Par 4	Par 3	Par 5	Par 4	Par 4	Par 36

HOW TO GET THERE

⬛iles south of St Andrews on the
⬛7 to Crail.

Kingsbarns
Golf Links

OLD COURSE HOTEL
St ANDREWS
GOLF RESORT & SPA

Located in the heart of the home of golf, the hotel is stunningly situated overlooking the infamous 17th Road Hole and the historic Royal and Ancient Clubhouse.

Just step through the entrance to discover why the Old Course Hotel has been described as one of Europe's leading resort hotels.

Residents will also enjoy privileges at the Duke's Course including a reduction in green fees and the opportunity to reserve tee-times when booking hotel accommodation.

Complimentary transport to Kingsbarns provided for residents.

For further information contact:
RESORT RESERVATIONS, OLD COURSE HOTEL, GOLF RESORT & SPA, ST ANDREWS,
KINGDOM OF FIFE KY16 9SP
TELEPHONE: (01334) 474371   FAX: (01334) 477668

Lundin

Golf beside the sea, or a game inland? Sometimes, especially when the weather is unsettled, it can be a difficult choice. Links golf is the original and many would say, finest type of golf, but to be toyed with by the wind for 18 consecutive holes in a completely exposed environment isn't everyone's idea of heaven.

For those links enthusiasts seeking a (hopefully temporary) change of scenery there are a handful of good inland courses in Fife - Ladybank is the best - but another suggestion is to visit Lundin Golf Club. Situated beside the shores of Largo Bay, one might imagine this to be a links course - to an extent it is precisely this, although nine of the holes also possess distinctly inland characteristics.

A round of golf at Lundin starts and finishes close to the sea. In between times the layout journeys inland, a change of mood signalled by the appearance and bisecting nature of an old railway line. The turf hereabouts is slightly softer and there are several trees which provide a degree of protection from the elements; gorse or whin bushes are also present, adding a dash of colour in season.

Designed by James Braid, Lundin has a wealth of strong holes. When the Open is played at St Andrews the course invariably hosts a Final Qualifying event. The long par four 4th is often singled out as best hole; it is not a hole for the timid for a hooked tee shot here will land on the beach and a weak approach will likely finish in the burn that meanders in front of the green.

COURSE INFORMATION & FACILITIES

Lundin Golf Club
Golf Road, Lundin Links
Fife. KY8 6BA

Secretary: D.R.Thomson
Tel: 01333 320202. Fax: 01333 329743.

Golf Professional: D.K.Webster
Tel: 01333 320051.

Green Fees:
Weekdays - £29, Weekends - £37(Sat pm -Round only)
Weekdays (day) - £37.
Some time restrictions.

CARD OF THE COURSE – PAR 71

1	2	3	4	5	6	7	8	9	Out
424	346	335	452	140	330	273	364	555	3219
Par 4	Par 4	Par 4	Par 4	Par 3	Par 4	Par 4	Par 4	Par 5	Par 36
10	11	12	13	14	15	16	17	18	In
353	466	150	512	175	418	314	345	442	3512
Par 4	Par 4	Par 3	Par 5	Par 3	Par 4	Par 4	Par 4	Par 4	Par 36

HOW TO GET THERE

miles east of Leven, on the
915 Kirkcaldy to St Andrews
ad. Take any of
e roads leading
the sea in the
llage of Lundin
nks.

Lundin
Golf Club

Machrihanish

Situated on the south western tip of the Mull of Kintyre, Machrihanish is perhaps the most geographically remote of all the great courses in the British Isles. And yet, if ever a journey was worth the effort …..

For the lover of traditional links golf, Machrihanish has everything. The layout has altered quite a bit since the late 19th century when it was designed by 'Old' Tom Morris, but the natural character of the course remains. Not only are the fairways among the most naturally undulating in the British Isles, but the greens are some of the most amazingly contoured – awkward stances and blind shots are very much a feature of Machrihanish.

There is nothing blind, however, about the course's legendary opening hole – from the tee the challenge ahead is very visible. It is a long par four of 423 yards and the only way of ensuring that the green can be reached in two shots is by hitting a full-blooded drive across the waters of Machrihanish Bay. From the back tees a 200 yard carry is called for. 'Intimidating' is the description: 'Death or Glory' is the result.

After the 1st the rest must be easy? Not a chance! If the opening hole tests the drive, several of the following holes will test the approach shot, particularly perhaps the 2nd, 7th and 14th. Machrihanish has its own 'Postage Stamp' hole, the 4th – just 123 yards – and there are successive short holes at the 15th and 16th. The course starts to wind down at the 17th and pars here are frequently followed by birdies at the 18th and, of course, considerable celebration at the 19th.

COURSE INFORMATION & FACILITIES

The Machrihanish Golf Club
Machrihanish, Campbeltown
Argyll PA28 6PT

Secretary: Anna Anderson.
Tel: 01586 810213. Fax: 01586-810221.

Golf Professional Ken Campbell
Tel: 01586-810277. (for bookings)

Green Fees: Weekdays + Sun – £25.
Sat – £30.
Weekdays (day) + Sun – £40. Saturday (day) – £50.
Some time restrictions.

CARD OF THE COURSE – PAR 70

1	2	3	4	5	6	7	8	9	Out
428	394	374	122	385	301	428	339	353	3124
Par 4	Par 4	Par 4	Par 3	Par 4	Par 4	Par 4	Par 4	Par 4	Par 35
10	11	12	13	14	15	16	17	18	In
503	197	513	370	438	168	231	368	313	3101
Par 5	Par 3	Par 5	Par 4	Par 4	Par 3	Par 3	Par 4	Par 4	Par 35

HOW TO GET THERE

pproximately three hours
rive from Glasgow. The
ost direct route is by the
82 to Tarbet on Loch
omond, then the A83 via
veraray and Lochgilphead.

Machrihanish
Golf Club

Montrose

Montrose is one of the hidden gems of Scottish golf. Its qualities may be sufficiently appreciated for it to be a regular host of important amateur events, but Montrose is nowhere near as widely acclaimed as it should be.

It is a classic links, and an ancient one at that. The Medal Course at Montrose is the fifth oldest golf course in the world – golf was played over this turf in the 16th century. During the mid 1800s, at a time when only a handful of clubs possessed 18 holes, Montrose boasted 25!

Montrose's proximity to Carnoustie is a major reason why holidaying golfers tend to overlook the links; to do so, however, is to miss out on a golf course that encapsulates the charm and unpredictability of links golf. (As a publicly

managed facility, the green fees are also remarkably good value.)

The course lays down the gauntlet on the opening hole, an uphill par four that requires two accurate shots to find the green. The 2nd tee overlooks a vast sandy beach and the hole features an extraordinary rippling fairway. The short 3rd is called 'Table', and if you fail to land your tee shot on the putting surface, your next shot could be extremely difficult. The 4th is another characterful hole, rivalling the long 9th as the best par four on the front nine. Overall the terrain is slightly less interesting on the back nine, although the green at the 16th is wildly contoured, and the 17th, with its magnificently angled shelf green may be the best hole of the entire round.

CARD OF THE COURSE – PAR 71

1	2	3	4	5	6	7	8	9	Out
393	388	155	365	292	490	370	331	443	3227
Par 4	Par 4	Par 3	Par 4	Par 4	Par 5	Par 4	Par 4	Par 4	Par 36

10	11	12	13	14	15	16	17	18	In
379	441	150	320	416	542	233	416	346	3243
Par 4	Par 4	Par 3	Par 4	Par 4	Par 5	Par 3	Par 4	Par 4	Par 35

HOW TO GET THERE

ontrose lies 35 miles from
undee and 40 miles from
berdeen Airport. By road
om the south follow the
90, turn off at Brechin and
llow the A935 to Montrose.

Montrose
Golf Club

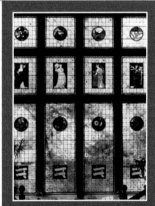

Moray

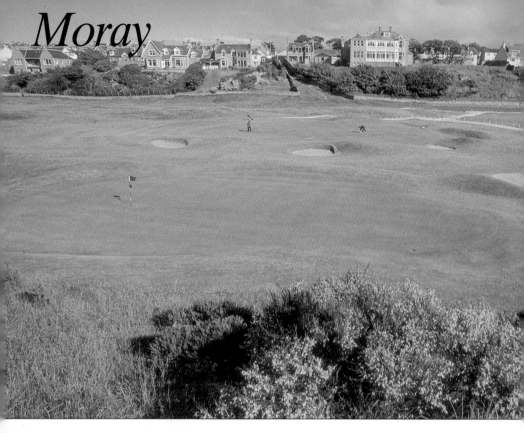

Which is the finest finishing hole in Scotland? Disciples of St Andrews would say it has to be the 18th on the Old Course, largely on the basis that it would be heresy to contemplate any other. Nick Faldo thinks it's to be found at Muirfield, but then since he's won two Open Championships there he may be a little biased. At the risk of being damned or disagreeing with Britain's greatest ever golfer, I'll advance the cause of Lossiemouth; or to be more precise, the 18th on the Old Course at the Moray Golf Club in Lossiemouth.

For anyone living south of the border, Lossiemouth is a long journey. Fortunately there are many attractions besides the above mentioned. Morayshire the county has much appeal. This is whisky country and the scenery is spectacular. As for Moray Golf Club, it has an additional 35 holes to savour.

Old Tom Morris laid out the original course in 1889. A second course - initially nine holes but later extended to 18 - was built in 1909 at a time when Lossiemouth was one of Scotland's most fashionable golfing resorts. Today anyone on a pilgrimage to Royal Dornoch via Nairn should consider adding an extra day's golf to their itinerary.

Essentially an 'out and back' layout, the inward nine of the Old Course returns along the shore. The last five holes reveal the best of the links, including of course, that marvellous finishing hole; here an elevated green nestling in the dunes presents a perfect golfing stage.

COURSE INFORMATION & FACILITIES

Moray Golf Club
Stotfield Road, Lossiemouth,
Moray. IV31 6QS

Secretary: Boyd Russell
Tel: 01343 812018. Fax: 01343 815102.

Golf Professional: Alistair Thomson
Tel: 01343 813330.

Green Fees:
Weekdays - £30, Weekends - £40.
Weekdays (day) - £40, Weekends (day) - £50
Handicap certificate required.

CARD OF THE COURSE – PAR 71

1	2	3	4	5	6	7	8	9	Out
332	494	397	197	416	145	434	452	310	3177
Par 4	Par 5	Par 4	Par 3	Par 4	Par 3	Par 4	Par 4	Par 4	Par 35

10	11	12	13	14	15	16	17	18	In
312	423	389	415	409	184	351	506	406	3395
Par 4	Par 4	Par 4	Par 4	Par 4	Par 3	Par 4	Par 5	Par 4	Par 36

HOW TO GET THERE

miles North of Elgin. Follow
6 from Aberdeen or Inveresss,
ke turn off for Lossiemouth in
gin.

erdeen - 90 mins.
verness - 45 mins.
airn - 30 mins.

Moray
Golf Club

Murcar

yrshire, Fife and Lothian may be
more obvious locations for a links
golfing holiday, but the North East
of Scotland - the Grampian region, if you
like - shouldn't be overlooked. Aberdeen
is the major city here and it has much to
offer in the way of quality links golf. In
particular two outstanding links courses
lie adjacent to one another just north of
the city (on the same side as the Airport),
namely Royal Aberdeen and Murcar.
And some 45 minutes drive north of these
two championship links is Cruden Bay,
'the Ballybunion of Scotland.'

Royal Aberdeen is better known than
Murcar; how much this has to do with the
former's 'Royal' prefix is hard to judge,
but on a hole-by-hole analysis many
consider Murcar to be its equal. In any

event, both are decidedly worth
investigating.

Established in 1909, Murcar is an
uncompromising links. It's not long, but
it's tough. According to Golf Monthly
writer, Barry Ward, "the faiways are
tighter than a taxman's purse and
hemmed with fearsome rough." The
terrain is fairly undulating throughout -
some fairways are decidedly humpy and
hillocky - and there are one or two blind
shots. Several tees are elevated and
provide impressive sea views.

The par four 7th is the best and most
exhilarating hole at Murcar. From a high
tee overlooking the shore, you must drive
over a burn and then thread your second
shot between dunes to a well defended
plateau green.

COURSE INFORMATION & FACILITIES

Murcar Golf Club
Bridge of Don
Aberdeen AB23 8BD.

Secretary: David Corstorphine.
Tel: 01224 704354.

Golf Professional Gary Forbes Tel: 01224 704370.

Green Fees:
Weekdays – £30. Weekends – £35.
Weekdays (day) – £40. Weekends (day) – £45.
Handicap certificates required. Some time restrictions.

CARD OF THE COURSE – PAR 71

1	2	3	4	5	6	7	8	9	Out
322	367	401	489	162	447	423	383	323	3317
Par 4	Par 4	Par 4	Par 5	Par 3	Par 4	Par 4	Par 4	Par 4	Par 36

10	11	12	13	14	15	16	17	18	In
402	338	155	386	482	351	160	367	329	2970
Par 4	Par 4	Par 3	Par 4	Par 5	Par 4	Par 3	Par 4	Par 4	Par 35

HOW TO GET THERE

prox 5 miles from centre
Aberdeen to N.E. off A92
terhead/Fraserburgh Road.

Murcar
Golf Club

Nairn

Nairn's championship links nestles on the southern shores of the Moray Firth, approximately 15 miles due east of Inverness. It enjoys a serene, picturesque setting. Mind you, things haven't always been quite so peaceful in this part of the world. It was not far from here, in 1746, that the bloody Battle of Culloden took place; and, in even more ancient times, nearby Cawdor Castle was the setting for several scenes (and many dastardly deeds) in Shakespeare's play, Macbeth.

Fortunately there is no semblance of wickedness about the golf course. What you see at Nairn is what you get. (And the best time to see it, incidentally, is in early summer when the gorse – or whins – are in bloom, turning the links from green to gold.) Nairn is not the longest of championship courses, nor it is an architectural classic in the Royal Dornoch mould, however it unfailingly provides an interesting, varied and decidedly attractive challenge; it is a course that rewards good strategy, accuracy and sound judgement of distance.

The first seven holes run close to the sea. The best in this sequence may be the 3rd and 5th, both are elegant, medium length par fours. In time honoured links fashion, the course turns about-face at the 10th (an outstanding par five) and, with the exception of holes 13 to 15 which spear inland, heads steadily home.

Nairn has hosted many important events over the years, including the 1994 British Amateur Championship and the 37th Walker Cup in 1999.

HOW TO GET THERE

6 — Inverness to Nairn
6 miles) turn left down
abank Road.
6 — to Nairn (88 miles)
n right down Seabank
ad.

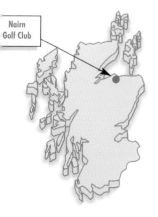

Nairn
Golf Club

COURSE INFORMATION & FACILITIES

The Nairn Golf Club
Seabank Road,
Nairn. IV12 41HB

Secretary: James G.Somerville.
Tel: 01667 453208. Fax: 01667 456328.

Golf Professional Robin P.Fyfe.

Green Fees:
Weekdays – £55. Weekends – £60.
Handicap certificate required. Some time restrictions.

CARD OF THE COURSE – PAR 72

1	2	3	4	5	6	7	8	9	Out
400	499	400	146	390	185	552	359	358	3289
Par 4	Par 5	Par 4	Par 3	Par 4	Par 3	Par 5	Par 4	Par 4	Par 36

10	11	12	13	14	15	16	17	18	In
540	163	445	435	221	309	424	364	555	3456
Par 5	Par 3	Par 4	Par 4	Par 3	Par 4	Par 4	Par 4	Par 5	Par 36

North Berwick

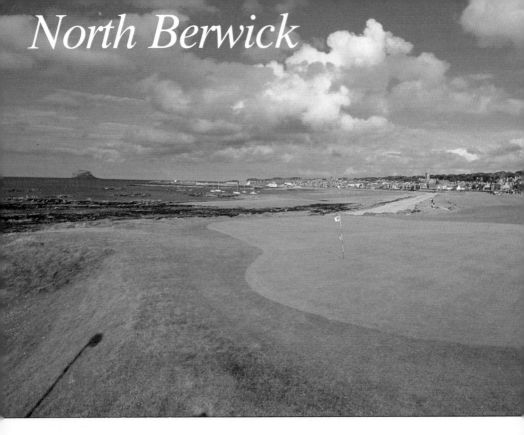

The golfer who journeys to Ayrshire essentially to inspect the links at Turnberry and Troon, but discovers that he actually prefers Prestwick, is the same player who visits Muirfield (and, yes, enjoys the challenge) but falls in love with the West Links at North Berwick.

For one thing, North Berwick's setting is one of the most captivating in golf. The first three holes on the West Links run adjacent to the shore, as, broadly speaking, do the 10th to the 14th on the inward nine – the course being laid out in the shape of a figure of eight. The Forth Estuary is on the golfer's right-hand side as he plays the opening holes: Bass Rock, a miniature Ailsa Craig, and a host of rocky islets command attention, as does a great sweep of sandy beach. But it is the golf itself that especially captivates.

The character (and occasional eccentricities) of the links are immediately apparent. The opening tee shot is invariably played with a long iron in order to lay up short of a deep gully; this is followed by a semi-blind second to a green that occupies a craggy hilltop and slopes sharply towards the sea. The drive at the 2nd must flirt with the shore, and at the 3rd the approach is hit over an ancient stone wall that traverses the fairway.

The finest sequence occurs between the 12th and 16th. Here one must confront the original 'Redan' hole, North Berwick's classic and much imitated par three 15th, and, at the next, the most mischievously contoured green in golf.

COURSE INFORMATION & FACILITIES

North Berwick West Links
The New Club House, Beach Road,
North Berwick, East Lothian. EH39 4BB

Secretary: A.G.Flood
Tel: 01620 895040.

Golf Professional: D.Huish Tel: 01620 892135.

Green Fees:
Weekdays - £36, Weekends - £54,
Weekdays (day) - £54. Weekends (day) - £72.
Letter of introduction and handicap certificate required.
Some time restrictions.

CARD OF THE COURSE – PAR 71

1	2	3	4	5	6	7	8	9	Out
328	431	464	175	373	162	354	495	510	3292
Par 4	Par 4	Par 4	Par 3	Par 4	Par 3	Par 4	Par 5	Par 5	Par 36

10	11	12	13	14	15	16	17	18	In
176	550	389	365	376	192	381	425	274	3128
Par 3	Par 5	Par 4	Par 4	Par 4	Par 3	Par 4	Par 4	Par 4	Par 35

HOW TO GET THERE

om A1 follow signs to
orth Berwick. Course
tuated on west side of town.

North Berwick
West Links

Prestwick

restwick is the original home of the original major championship. For this reason alone the famous Ayrshire links demands inspection; but there are many other compelling reasons.

Critics occasionally deride Prestwick, condemning it as a golfing anachronism: 'You'd never build a course like that nowadays', they sneer. 'More's the pity', is my immediate response; but in any event, Prestwick continues to inspire some of the world's leading modern-day architects. (Ask Pete Dye how he became so besotted with rail-road ties and pot bunkers!)

There were only 12 holes at Prestwick when the first Open Championship was contested in 1860. The competitors played 36 holes – three rounds in a day – and the first winner was Willie Park. Old Tom Morris, who had laid out the course in the early 1850s, won four of the next six Opens (the first 12 were held at Prestwick) and his son, Young Tom Morris, then won four of the next five.

Today there are of course 18 holes at Prestwick, yet seven of the original twelve greens are included in the current layout. So you really can walk in the footsteps of Old Tom and Young Tom. And much of the character of the course has been retained. Golfers still play over humps and hillocks, confront blind shots over alarmingly large bunkers – 'the Cardinal' and 'the Alps' remain fully intact – and putt on some of the most mischievously contoured greens in golf. Prestwick isn't an anachronism - it's bliss.

AYRSHIRE

COURSE INFORMATION & FACILITIES

Prestwick Golf Club
2 Links Road
Ayrshire. KA9 1QG

Secretary: Ian T Bunch
Tel: 01292 477404.

Golf Professional: Frank C Rennie
Tel: 01292 479483.

Green Fees:
Weekdays (Round) - £75, Weekdays (day) - £100.
Letter of introduction and handicap certificate required.
Some time restrictions.

CARD OF THE COURSE – PAR 71

1	2	3	4	5	6	7	8	9	Out
346	167	482	382	206	362	430	431	444	3250
Par 4	Par 3	Par 5	Par 4	Par 3	Par 4	Par 4	Par 4	Par 4	Par 35

10	11	12	13	14	15	16	17	18	In
454	195	513	460	362	347	288	391	284	3294
Par 4	Par 3	Par 5	Par 4	Par 4	Par 4	Par 4	Par 4	Par 4	Par 36

HOW TO GET THERE

ext to Prestwick railway
ation,. 30 miles South of
lasgow, just off M77.

Prestwick
Golf Club

Royal Aberdeen

Founded in 1780, Royal Aberdeen is the sixth oldest golf club in the world. For the first 35 years of its existence the club was known as The Society of Golfers at Aberdeen, with membership of the society being determined by ballot. They were clearly a fastidious group of gentlemen, for in 1783 they became the first to introduce the five minute limit on searching for lost golf balls.

Although not the longest of Scotland's championship links, Royal Aberdeen is very exposed to the elements and the wind can often make a mockery of some of the distances as indicated on the score card. There is also a considerable spread of gorse to contend with – or avoid – and the rough can be very punishing. It might

also be mentioned that there are nearly one hundred bunkers, many of which are deep pot bunkers – the par three 8th being surrounded by ten of them!

The course has a traditional 'out and back' layout, the front nine hugging the shore, and the back nine returning on the landward side. The outward nine is definitely the more interesting of the two halves. The eminent Scottish golf writer Sam McKinlay was moved to remark: 'There are few courses in these islands with a better, more testing, more picturesque outward nine.' However, the most difficult hole on the course is possibly the last hole – a lengthy par four, well bunkered and usually played into the teeth of the prevailing wind.

COURSE INFORMATION & FACILITIES

Royal Aberdeen Golf Club, Balgownie Links
Links Road, Bridge of Don,
Aberdeen

Director of Golf: Ronnie Macaskill
Tel: 01224 702571. Fax: 01224 826591.

Golf Professional: Ronnie Macaskill Tel: 01224 702221.

Green Fees:
Weekdays - £55, Weekends -£65.
Weekdays (day) - £75.
Letter of introduction and Handicap certificate required.
Some time restrictions.

CARD OF THE COURSE – PAR 70

1	2	3	4	5	6	7	8	9	Out
409	530	223	423	326	486	375	147	453	3372
Par 4	Par 5	Par 3	Par 4	Par 4	Par 5	Par 4	Par 3	Par 4	Par 36

10	11	12	13	14	15	16	17	18	In
342	166	383	375	390	341	389	180	434	3512
Par 4	Par 3	Par 4	Par 4	Par 4	Par 4	Par 4	Par 3	Par 4	Par 34

HOW TO GET THERE

e club is situated on the north
de of the city of Aberdeen,
eyond the mouth of the river
on. Northbound on
e main road from
erdeen motorists
ould turn right at
e traffic lights after
e bridge into
nks Road,
rk left
) yards
.

Royal Aberdeen
Golf Club

Where several birdies are par for the course

EACH year, around 1000 golfers migrate for a golf break at the Udny Arms Hotel, and it isn't difficult to understand why. With the Forvie Nature Reserve as a backdrop to our local 100 year old course, and Royal Aberdeen, Murcar, Newmachar and Cruden Bay only 15 minutes away, the Udny Arms is a natural place to rest and eat.

THE TASTE OF SCOTLAND

To find out why our golfing visitors can't help returning, call Jennifer Craig on: 01358 789444

Udny Arms
HOTEL
ON THE YTHAN

UDNY ARMS HOTEL, MAINS STREET, NEWBURGH
ABERDEENSHIRE AB41 OBL
TEL: 01358 789444, FAX: 01358 789012
E-MAIL: enquiry@udny.demon.co.uk

107

Royal Dornoch

*D*ornoch is a magical place. It was here in the 18th century that Janet Horne, 'the last witch in Scotland' was summarily executed. And Royal Dornoch would appear to be a magical links, for it has long been casting a spell over some of the greatest golfers who ever lived.

Dornoch is geographically challenged. It is 50 miles beyond Inverness and 600 miles from London; but this fact didn't deter the Great Triumvirate, Messrs. Vardon, Taylor and Braid from visiting the links in the early years of this century. Nor did it discourage Joyce Wethered who made regular trips from the South of England. In more recent times, Tom Watson, Ben Crenshaw, Greg Norman and Nick Faldo have all embarked on what is a seemingly irresistible pilgrimage.

So what is the charm of Royal Dornoch? Firstly, there is the setting. Dornoch may be 'miles from anywhere' but this merely adds to the mystique. The links is bordered by the Dornoch Firth and a sweep of pristine white sand. Much of the golf course is blanketed in gorse and when this flowers in early summer it is a glorious sight. Then there's Dornoch's remarkable history. It is the third oldest links in the world; golf has been played here since the early 1600s.

Finally there's the quality and character of the links itself. Dornoch is often described as the most natural golf course in the world. Renowned for its magnificently contoured greens, many of which sit on natural plateaux, the golf course flows wonderfully from tee to green. Yes, Dornoch is a classic, as well as enchanting links.

HOW TO GET THERE

5 miles north of Inverness
ff A9. 1-2 miles after
ornoch Firth Bridge.
urn right off town square
hen after 100 yards turn
ft to Clubhouse.

Royal Dornoch
Golf Club

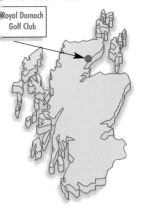

COURSE INFORMATION & FACILITIES

Royal Dornoch Golf Club
Golf Road
Dornoch IV25 3LW.

Secretary: John S. Duncan.
Tel: 01862 810219. Fax: 01862 810792.

Golf Professional: Andrew Skinner
Tel: 01862 810902. Fax: 01862 811095.

Green Fees:
Weekdays (Apr - Oct) – £55. Weekdays (Nov - Mar) – £40.
Weekends (Apr - Oct) – £65. Weekends (Nov - Mar) – £45.
Handicap certificates required. Some time restrictions.
Saturdays members only.

CARD OF THE COURSE – PAR 70

1	2	3	4	5	6	7	8	9	Out
331	184	414	427	354	163	463	437	529	3302
Par 4	Par 3	Par 4	Par 4	Par 4	Par 3	Par 4	Par 4	Par 5	Par 35

10	11	12	13	14	15	16	17	18	In
177	450	557	180	445	358	402	405	456	3430
Par 3	Par 4	Par 5	Par 3	Par 4	Par 4	Par 4	Par 4	Par 4	Par 35

Royal Troon

When one daydreams of Royal Troon, one pictures vast Ayrshire skies, fierce winds blowing off the sea from the Mull of Kintyre and, quite probably, a 71 year old golfer in plaid plus twos punching a five iron into the wind and into the hole at the par three 8th.

It is difficult to think of Troon without thinking of the 'Postage Stamp', as the short 8th on the Old Course is known. And it is almost impossible to reflect on the 'Postage Stamp' without recalling Gene Sarazen's televised hole-in-one in the 1973 British Open.

As one of eight courses presently on the Open Championship rota, Troon has seen much drama over the years. Like Royal Lytham in Lancashire, it has proven a happy hunting ground for American golfers: the last five Opens at Troon have been claimed by Messrs Palmer, Weiskopf, Watson, Calcavecchia and, most recently in 1997, by Justin Leonard.

Troon is a windswept, traditional 'out and back' links. Apart from the first three holes which run adjacent to the shore and are fairly benign, it is uncompromisingly rugged: Troon has even been described as 'golf's ultimate battleground'! The links has both the longest hole of any Open course – the par five 6th, and the shortest – the Postage Stamp. In the par four 11th, it also possesses one of the toughest, with its railway out-of-bounds and thick gorse. The finest two-shot hole, however, may be the 13th, which features an elevated drive to a wonderfully crumpled fairway.

HOW TO GET THERE

 miles from
estwickAirport. South East
 Troon on B749 from A77
avelling south from
asgow

Royal Troon
Golf Club

COURSE INFORMATION & FACILITIES

Royal Troon Golf Club
Craigend Road, Troon
Ayrshire KA10 6EP

Secretary: J.W.Chandler
Tel: 01292 311555. Fax: 01292 318204.

Golf Professional: R.B.Anderson Tel: 01292 313281.

Green Fees:
Weekdays – £N/A. Weekdays (day) – £115.
Letter of introduction and handicap certificate required.
Some time restrictions.

CARD OF THE COURSE – PAR 71

1	2	3	4	5	6	7	8	9	Out
357	381	371	522	194	544	381	123	387	3260
Par 4	Par 4	Par 4	Par 5	Par 3	Par 5	Par 4	Par 3	Par 4	Par 36

10	11	12	13	14	15	16	17	18	In
385	421	427	411	175	445	533	210	374	3381
Par 4	Par 4	Par 4	Par 4	Par 3	Par 4	Par 5	Par 3	Par 4	Par 35

Southerness

*T*wo of Britain's greatest and least explored links courses stare at one another across the Solway Firth – one is on the English side at Silloth and the other lies north of the border at Southerness. As close as they appear on the map, the only way of travelling from one to the other is by a fairly lengthy drive around the coast via Gretna Green. Before the war a bridge crossed the Solway, but before the war Southerness didn't have a golf course.

Situated 16 miles south of Dumfries, Southerness is the only true championship links in Great Britain to have been built since 1945. Quite a contrast to Ireland where the likes of Tralee, Carne and The European have all been constructed within the last 20 years.

So golf came to Southerness about 500 years after it came to St Andrews, but one cannot help wondering why it took so long, after all, the much more remote golfing outposts of Dornoch and Machrihanish took root in the dim and distant past and a more natural and pleasanter site for the links it is hard to imagine. Sandy terrain, rampant heather, dense bracken and prickly golden gorse all present themselves in abundance here; as for that matter do firm, fast fairways and subtly contoured greens.

The 12th is undoubtedly the best hole a Southerness: a well positioned drive here is essential as the second shot must be fired towards a narrow green which sits on a plateau and looks down over a beautiful beach; deep bunkers guard the green front right and a pond will gleefully swallow any shot that strays left of centre.

COURSE INFORMATION & FACILITIES

Southerness Golf Club
Kirkbean
Dumfries DG2 8AZ.

Secretary: A. Robin.
Tel: 01387 880677. Fax: 01387 880644.

Green Fees:
Weekdays – £32. Weekends – £45.
Weekdays (day) – £32. Weekends (day) – £45.
Handicap certificates required.

DUMFRIES

CARD OF THE COURSE – PAR 69

1	2	3	4	5	6	7	8	9	Out
393	450	408	169	496	405	215	371	435	3342
Par 4	Par 4	Par 4	Par 3	Par 5	Par 4	Par 3	Par 4	Par 4	Par 35

10	11	12	13	14	15	16	17	18	In
168	390	421	467	458	217	433	175	495	3224
Par 3	Par 4	Par 4	Par 4	Par 4	Par 3	Par 4	Par 3	Par 5	Par 34

HOW TO GET THERE

ave A75 at Dumfries and
llow A710 signposted
lway Coast and follow for
5 miles south. Southerness
signposted (approx. 1 mile).

Southerness
Golf Club

St Andrews (Old Course)

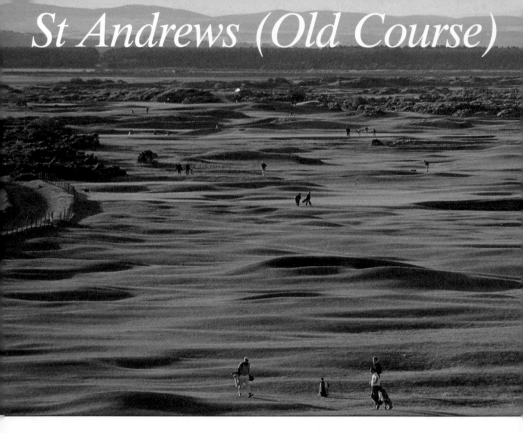

*I*s the Old Course at St Andrews, to adopt the title of this guide, 'the best links in the British Isles'? Is it the finest course in the world? Those who rank golf courses must consider the claims of St Andrews more than any other. The reason is simple enough: St Andrews is the mother of all golf courses. It is the oldest links in the world – golf was being played there long before Christopher Columbus discovered America.

It is a mother in another sense. Historically, spiritually and architecturally, every golf course owes something, if not its very existence, to the Old Course at St Andrews. To a degree, it has inspired and influenced every course that has ever been built. So while there may be more beautiful courses, more difficult ones, and some that are deemed more interesting, or more stimulating to play, is there really a greater course than St Andrews?

St Andrews is incomparable.

It is often suggested that a good test of a golf course's quality is the extent to which, after the first time of playing, you are able to remember each hole. This is not so easy at St Andrews given that the first time you visit the Old Course you are likely to be so overwhelmed by the sense of history that you play the links in a semi-trance. You will probably recall the outstanding features of the layout – the huge double greens, the myriad pot bunkers, the Swilcan Burn etc. – but with the exception of the 1st, the 17th and the 18th, it may prove difficult to recall or distinguish individual holes.

The 17th at St Andrews is perhaps the most famous and most feared par four in golf. 'It's never over', commentators always remark, 'until the Road Hole has been successfully negotiated.'

CARD OF THE COURSE – PAR 72

1	2	3	4	5	6	7	8	9	Out
370	411	352	419	514	374	359	166	307	3272
Par 4	Par 4	Par 4	Par 4	Par 5	Par 4	Par 4	Par 3	Par 4	Par 36

10	11	12	13	14	15	16	17	18	In
318	172	316	398	523	401	351	461	354	3512
Par 4	Par 3	Par 4	Par 4	Par 5	Par 4	Par 4	Par 4	Par 4	Par 36

HOW TO GET THERE

ᵽm Edinburgh and the south:
vel north on the M90 over the Forth
dge. Leave the motorway at junction
nd follow the A92 to its junction with
A914 north of Glenrothes. Take the
14 to the next roundabout, turn right
d continue on the A91 through
ᵽar to St Andrews.
ᵽm Perth and the North: Travel
th on the M90 and exit at
ction 7. Drive through
nathort and continue
the A91 through
htermuchty
d Cuper
ᵽt
drews.

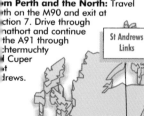

St Andrews
Links

The Machrie

Scotland is famous for many things, and two of its greatest gifts to mankind are golf and whisky. The origins of each are uncertain, lost in the mists of time, but a place where both can be sampled in their purest form is on the Hebridean island of Islay. This is the home of Laphroaig, Bowmore, Bunnahabhainn and, yes, The Machrie Golf Club.

You can fly to Islay from Glasgow (a 35 minute flight) or you can drive halfway down the Kintyre peninsula and take a two hour ferry journey to Port Ellen - it depends how quickly you wish to prepare yourself for another world.

Machrie does seem caught in a golfing timewarp. Here is where you half expect to bump into Old Tom Morris. It is an old fashioned links course and is set amid gorgeous and spectacular surroundings.

There are at least a dozen blind shots at Machrie, so those who like their golf laid out on a plate are advised not to board the ferry or the plane. There are several sunken greens and elevated tees; most of the fairways twist and tumble violently and occasionally you are required to play shots that you are unlikely to face on any other golf course.

If asked to select the best holes at Machrie you might pick the 3rd, the 6th, the 7th and the 13th. But, really, the entire golf links is unforgettable.

HOW TO GET THERE

plane from Glasgow Airport, flight time
minutes. By ferry from Kennacraig,
yll, crossing time 2 hours Glasgow is
ut 110 miles by road from Kennacraig.
course is minutes from each terminal
rtesy coach will collect hotel
dents.

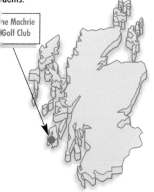

he Machrie
Golf Club

COURSE INFORMATION & FACILITIES

The Machrie Hotel & Golf Links
Port Ellen, Isle of Islay
Argyll PA42 7AN.

Manager: Ian Brown.
Tel: 01496 302310. Fax: 01496 302404.

Green Fees: Non-residents
Weekdays (ends) – £25.
Weekdays (day) – £32.50.
Some time restrictions.

CARD OF THE COURSE – PAR 71

1	2	3	4	5	6	7	8	9	Out
308	508	319	390	163	344	395	337	392	3156
Par 4	Par 5	Par 4	Par 4	Par 3	Par 4	Par 4	Par 4	Par 4	Par 36

10	11	12	13	14	15	16	17	18	In
156	357	174	488	423	335	411	352	374	3070
Par 3	Par 4	Par 3	Par 5	Par 4	Par 4	Par 4	Par 4	Par 4	Par 35

Turnberry

A quarter of a century ago it was said that the golfing visitor to Scotland journeyed to St Andrews for the history, and to Turnberry for the beauty. Nowadays this is only partially true.

Consider: 'the Duel in the Sun' – Nicklaus v Watson in 1977; Greg Norman's 63 in the wind in 1986; and Nick Price's eagle putt in 1994. Turnberry's golfing history has begun to reflect the magnificence of its setting.

There are of course 36 holes at Turnberry, with the Ailsa and the Arran Courses. The latter is a worthy challenge, but it is the Ailsa that everyone wants to play. As beautifully maintained as Muirfield, it features a litany of memorable holes. Perhaps it is not as breathtakingly rugged as one or two great links – there are no giant sand hills and no spectacular changes in elevation, but then Turnberry is breathtaking in a different way.

After three holes 'inland', as it were, the Ailsa Course hugs the shore for a series of dramatic challenges between the 4th and 11th. The most celebrated holes are undoubtedly the 9th and 10th. The former is played adjacent to Turnberry Lighthouse, built over the remains of Turnberry Castle, birthplace of Robert the Bruce. The championship tee is perched on a pinnacle of rock with the sea crashing below. Play this hole and the wonderfully curving 10th and you can appreciate why comparisons are so often drawn between Turnberry and Pebble Beach.

miles north of Girvan on A77

Turnberry
Golf Club

COURSE INFORMATION & FACILITIES

Turnberry Hotel Golf Course and Spa
Turnberry
Ayrshire KA26 9LT

Director of Golf: Brian Gunson
Tel: 01655 331069. Fax: 01655 334043.

Golf Professional: David Fleming
Tel: 01655 331069. Fax: 01655 334043.

Green Fees:
Weekdays – £90. Weekends – £90.
Letter of introduction and handicap certificate required.
Some time restrictions.

CARD OF THE COURSE – PAR 70

1	2	3	4	5	6	7	8	9	Out
350	430	462	165	442	231	529	431	454	3494
Par 4	Par 4	Par 4	Par 3	Par 4	Par 3	Par 5	Par 4	Par 4	Par 35

10	11	12	13	14	15	16	17	18	In
452	174	446	412	449	209	409	497	434	3350
Par 4	Par 3	Par 4	Par 4	Par 4	Par 3	Par 4	Par 5	Par 4	Par 35

Western Gailes

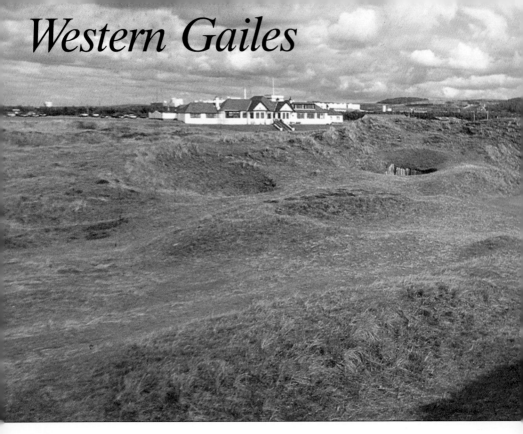

Sam McKinlay once commented, 'Western Gailes represents to the true golfer, to the connoisseur of the game, something approaching the ideal in golf'. Squeezed onto a narrow tract of land between the Atlantic Ocean and the Ayrshire coast's ubiquitous railway line, Western Gailes is indeed a marvellous and, in many ways, underrated links. It may not have the history of Prestwick (though the club celebrated its centenary in 1987), and the setting may not be as mouth-wateringly beautiful as Turnberry, nor does the links provide quite the stern, uncompromising challenge that is the hallmark of Royal Troon, but if a player wishes to experience a fine blend of all three then Western Gailes is the place to head for.

The 1st hole with its humpy, hillocky fairway, and its green heavily contoured and partially concealed in a dell could have been plucked from Prestwick. The long par four 2nd is bordered by the railway line – now you could be playing the 11th at Troon. And when you stand on the tee at the par three 7th (one of the great par threes in golf) and gaze out to sea at Ailsa Craig and the Isle of Arran, or along the coast, you could believe you were at Turnberry.

While Troon and the Ailsa Course at Turnberry are essentially 'out and back' layouts, at Western Gailes the clubhouse sits in the middle of the links. The golfer is lured away from the clubhouse for four holes and invited to play nine close to the sea before being reeled in from the 14th hole onwards.

HOW TO GET THERE

miles north of Troon (A78).
st off the A78/A71.

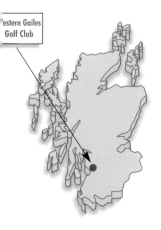

estern Gailes
Golf Club

COURSE INFORMATION & FACILITIES

Western Gailes Golf Club
Irvine
Ayrshire KA11 5AE

Secretary: Andrew M. McBean, C.A.
Tel: 01294 311649. Fax: 01294 312312.

Green Fees:
Weekdays – £60. Weekends – £70 (Sunday only).
Weekdays (day) – £90.
Letter of introduction and handicap certificate required.
Some time restrictions. No visitors on Thursdays or Saturdays.

CARD OF THE COURSE – PAR 71

1	2	3	4	5	6	7	8	9	Out
304	434	365	355	453	506	171	365	336	3289
Par 4	Par 4	Par 4	Par 4	Par 4	Par 5	Par 3	Par 4	Par 4	Par 36

10	11	12	13	14	15	16	17	18	In
348	445	436	141	562	194	404	443	377	3350
Par 4	Par 4	Par 4	Par 3	Par 5	Par 3	Par 4	Par 4	Par 4	Par 35

Powerscourt Gardens, Co. Wicklow

Ireland

*T*he Irish have long been telling the world that their links golf courses are just
as good as - if not better than - anything that Scotland has to offer. Until
quite recent times the rest of the world regarded this as a 'nice try', and
*nothing more than a bit of Irish blarney. But I did say 'until quite recent times'
because a growing number of commentators – from both sides of the Atlantic – have
begun to agree with the assessment. Here follows a few reasons for thinking the
impossible.*

*If you compare Scotland's 'Big Six', its finest or most famous half dozen courses with
their counterparts in Ireland, can you confidently say which collection is the more
impressive? Consider: St Andrews, Carnoustie, Muirfield, Turnberry, Royal Troon,
Royal Dornoch and Prestwick versus Ballybunion, Royal County Down, Royal
Portrush, Portmarnock, Lahinch and Rosses Point.*

*Scotland has the greater number of links courses and therefore it has been assumed
that it has much greater strength in depth. Where are the Irish equivalents of Nairn,
Western Gailes, Royal Aberdeen and Gullane, etc.? A few years ago even the most
optimistic Irish man would begin by offering Royal Dublin and Baltray as examples
and then, on searching for more names, quickly realise that he was on sticky ground.
However, while the map of Scottish links courses has barely changed in the last three
decades, Ireland's has altered dramatically.*

*During the 1970s and 1980s the south west of Ireland became a golfing Mecca, partly
because the Old Course at Ballybunion started to be hailed, by Tom Watson among
others, as 'the finest seaside course in the world'; partly because Waterville and Tralee
emerged on the scene, and partly because Ballybunion itself built a second 18 holes
in the dunes and now offered, 'the best 36 holes of links golf in the world.' No new
major links courses were built in Scotland during the `70s and `80s and yet, in
addition to the happenings in County Kerry, the west of Ireland unveiled three more
first class links courses, namely Connemara in County Galway, Murvagh in County
Donegal and Enniscrone in County Mayo. Then, in the north of Ireland, Portstewart,
which for so long had been completely overshadowed by Portrush, opened seven new*

holes that had been carved out of the most spectacular terrain imaginable, and suddenly it was being ranked among the top 30 links courses in the British Isles.

In the 1990s more and more golfing visitors poured into Ireland and the country began to challenge Scotland as Europe's number one golf holiday destination. In addition to the favourites, golfers began to discover such hidden jewels as The Island, Rosslare and Castlerock. More significantly, in the last decade alone, four outstanding new links have appeared in Ireland: The European Club, Portmarnock Hotel Links, Carne and Ballyliffin (Glashedy). Now which country has the stronger 'second string'?

As we begin the new Millennium, Scotland might seem to be 'fighting back' with the opening of the oh-so-impressive Kingsbarns, but the word is that Ireland may have yet one or two more amazing links courses in the pipeline. So, as they say, watch this space!

BALLYBUNION	PORTMARNOCK HOTEL LINKS
BALLYLIFFIN	PORTSTEWART
CARNE	ROSSLARE
CASTLEROCK	ROYAL COUNTY DOWN
CONNEMARA	ROYAL DUBLIN
COUNTY LOUTH	ROYAL PORTRUSH
COUNTY SLIGO	THE EUROPEAN
DONEGAL	THE ISLAND
ENNISCRONE	TRALEE
LAHINCH	WATERVILLE
PORTMARNOCK	

Ireland

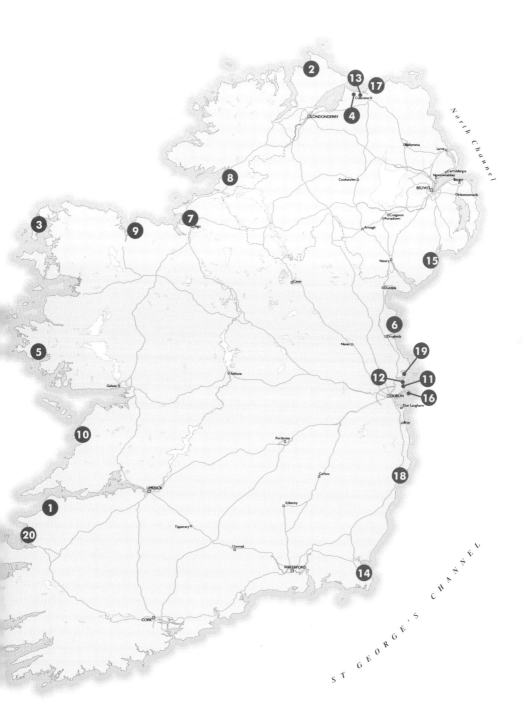

North Channel

St GEORGE'S CHANNEL

LONDONDERRY

BELFAST

Ballymena
Larne
Carrickfergus
Newtownabbey
Bangor
Newtownards

Coleraine

Cookstown

Craigavon
Portadown

Armagh

Newry

Dundalk

Cavan

Drogheda

Navan

DUBLIN
Dun Laoghaire
Bray

Athlone

Galway

Portlaoise

Carlow

Kilkenny

LIMERICK

Tipperary

Clonmel

WATERFORD

CORK

Ballybunion

*P*lease excuse the blasphemy, but for well-travelled golfers, particularly those with a penchant for seaside golf, Ballybunion is 'God's own Country.' In fact, mere mention of the name Ballybunion to such folk is enough to set their pulses racing.

The reason is simple enough. Situated in a remote but beautiful corner of County Kerry, Ballybunion is the most spectacular links on the planet. Thirty-six holes weave their way amidst – and occasionally carve a route through – the largest and most extensive range of sandhills in the British Isles. It is thrilling, swashbuckling golf. Moreover, one of the two 18 hole layouts, Ballybunion Old Course, is regarded by no lesser a judge than

Tom Watson as the world's greatest golf course. (The newer Cashen Course was designed by Robert Trent Jones and opened in the mid 1980s).

While the 2nd, 7th and 8th are marvellous holes, everyone remembers the back nine on the Old Course. And some golfers dream about the par four 11th. Bordered by huge dunes to the left and the Atlantic Ocean to the right, the fairway at this hole cascades down to a bunkerless green overlooking the sea.

The Old Course will host its first ever Irish Open Championship in June 2000. What a golden summer for golfers: a US Open at Pebble Beach, a British Open at St Andrews and an Irish Open at Ballybunion!

COURSE INFORMATION & FACILITIES

Ballybunion Golf Club
Sandhill Road,
Ballybunion, Co. Kerry.

Secretary: James J. McKenna.
Tel: 068-27146.

Golf Professional: Brian O'Callaghan Tel: 068-27842.

Green Fees:
Weekdays – IR£60. Weekends – IR£60.
Weekdays (day) – IR£80. Weekends (day) – IR£80.
Letter of introduction and handicap certificate required.
Time restrictions apply. Early booking available.

CARD OF THE COURSE (Old Course) – PAR 71

1	2	3	4	5	6	7	8	9	Out
392	445	220	520	524	364	432	153	454	3495
Par 4	Par 4	Par 3	Par 5	Par 5	Par 4	Par 4	Par 3	Par 4	Par 36

10	11	12	13	14	15	16	17	18	In
359	453	192	484	131	216	499	385	379	3098
Par 4	Par 4	Par 3	Par 5	Par 3	Par 3	Par 5	Par 4	Par 4	Par 35

HOW TO GET THERE

om Shannon Airport, take
ast road N69 to Ballybunion.
ne mile outside Ballybunion
the L106.

129

Ballyliffin

When a golf club is described as 'the Dornoch of Ireland' you can hardly ignore it; and when, on adding a further 18 holes that same club is christened 'the Ballybunion of the North', you are almost compelled to make a visit. Ballyliffin is the place in question and it is to be found near Malin Head on the northwestern tip of Donegal's Inishowen Peninsula.

It seems there were three reasons for the very flattering comparison with Royal Dornoch. Firstly, Ballyliffin's geography – Malin Head is the John O'Groats of Ireland and this is the country's most northerly situated golf club; secondly, the original 18 holes, now named the Old Links, is one of the world's most natural golf courses – its rippling fairways are especially fascinating; and thirdly, like Dornoch, Ballyliffin enjoys a remarkably beautiful and serene setting.

In 1995 Ballyliffin unveiled the Glashedy Links. Stretching to more than 7000 yards from the back tees and designed by Tom Craddock and Pat Ruddy, the new course is both formidable and thrilling to play. Writing in LINKS Magazine in November 1996, John Hopkins declared, "I have found the new Ballybunion." And he went on to suggest that the Glashedy Links "might be the best new links course to have been built this century."

'Almost compelled to make a visit'? How could you possibly think of missing Ballyliffin!

COURSE INFORMATION & FACILITIES

Ballyliffin Golf Club
Ballyliffin, Clonmany, Inishowen,
Co. Donegal.

Golf Office:
Tel: 00 353 77 76119. Fax: 00 353 77 76672.
e-mail:ballyliffingolfclub@tinet.ie

Green Fees:
Weekdays – IR£25. Weekends – IR£30.
Letter of introduction and handicap card required.
Restrictions apply on weekends.

CARD OF THE COURSE – PAR 72

1	2	3	4	5	6	7	8	9	Out
426	432	428	479	177	361	183	422	382	3290
Par 4	Par 4	Par 4	Par 5	Par 3	Par 4	Par 3	Par 4	Par 4	Par 35

10	11	12	13	14	15	16	17	18	In
397	419	448	572	183	440	426	549	411	3845
Par 4	Par 4	Par 4	Par 5	Par 3	Par 4	Par 4	Par 5	Par 4	Par 37

HOW TO GET THERE

ɔvelling from Belfast (and
 ɔrry) cross the Foyle Bridge
 d take the A2 towards
 ɔville, turning off for
 ɔrndonagh at Quigleys
 int/Carrowkeel. Ballyliffin
 ɔ miles beyond
 ɔrndonagh.

Carne

You often get the sense of complete isolation playing in Ireland, as if you are playing at the end of the earth, as far from civilisation as possible. Nowhere in Ireland is this sense more profound than at Carne. The nearest town, Ballina, is 30 miles away.

Carne is about as far west as you can get on mainland Ireland. Any further west and the Statue of Liberty would just about be visible. The course is situated on Mullet peninsula, on the edge of the Atlantic Ocean. Here you will find glorious views of Blacksod Bay and various islands out in the Atlantic.

Carne was built with one aim - to attract tourism. Those who have sampled its delights since the Eddie Hackett designed course was opened in 1993 have spread the word. Carne is worthy of trekking to this isolated part of County Mayo, and more golfers are doing so every year.

So natural is the linksland, that there is a feeling the course has been here for years. The greens, in particular, seem to belong to the land, as if the golfing greats have been pacing them since the turn of the century.

Huge sand dunes are the order of the day at Carne, and many are used to elevate the tees. This means that on most holes you can see the trouble that lies ahead. That's not to say you will avoid it, for the wind plays a big part in how well you play this course. Pray you get a calm day, otherwise you'll struggle to match your handicap. Just as well it only measures just over 6,600 yards.

COURSE INFORMATION & FACILITIES

Carne Golf Links
Carne, Belmullet
Co. Mayo.

Secretary Manager: Evelyn Keane Tel: 097 82292.
Fax: 097 81477.

Green Fees:
Weekdays – IR£22.   Weekends – IR£22.
Weekdays (day) – IR£22.   Weekends (day) – IR£22.

CARD OF THE COURSE – PAR 72

1	2	3	4	5	6	7	8	9	Out
366	183	376	473	378	363	162	365	327	2993
Par 4	Par 3	Par 4	Par 5	Par 4	Par 4	Par 3	Par 4	Par 4	Par 35

10	11	12	13	14	15	16	17	18	In
465	332	300	482	133	366	154	399	495	3126
Par 5	Par 4	Par 4	Par 5	Par 3	Par 4	Par 3	Par 4	Par 5	Par 37

HOW TO GET THERE

it N59 at Bangor Erris take
13 to Belmullet.

TEACH IORRAIS
—— H O T E L ——

*Teach Iorrais, stands amidst such a beautiful landscape and
provides the ideal venue for those seeking refuge from the
excesses of modern day living.*

*Within 15km of Teach Iorrais the renowned Carne Golf Links in
Belmullet, which is set on 260 acres of the most challenging
terrain. The hotel provides a bus shuttle service to and from this
18 hole Championship Links Course and preferential green fees
are available to guests.*

GEESALA, BALLINA, CO. MAYO
TEL:097 86888   FAX: 097 86855
EMAIL: teachior@iol.ie   www.teachiorrais.com

Castlerock

Not far from the glorious links of Royal Portrush, and where the River Bann enters the Atlantic Ocean, lies a gem of a links.

Castlerock Golf Club was founded back in 1901 when it was established as a nine hole layout. The club expanded the course to 18 holes in 1908, calling upon Ben Sayers to create a golf course worthy enough to sit near Portrush. Sayers is better known as a clubmaker, but the North Berwick man could also play. He participated in every Open Championship between 1880 and 1923, finishing second in 1888, third in 1889 and fifth in 1894.

While Sayers gave the game of golf clubs with names like the Jigger and the Dreadnought, perhaps his best contribution to golf architecture was to design the links at Castlerock. Good greens are the order of the day here. In the height of summer, when the course is hard and dry, the putting surfaces can be treacherously quick. Given that you often have to bounce the ball in on the approach shot, getting close to the flags calls for a delicate touch.

The best known hole at Castlerock is the 4th called 'Leg o' Mutton', a 200 yard par three with a railway line to the right, a burn on the left and a raised green. A three here is a good score as this is a green that is typically hard to hold. Among other outstanding holes at Castlerock are the par four 8th, the 9th (which is precisely the same length as the 4th) and, on the back nine, the exhilarating downhill par five 17th.

Revisions to Sayers' layout were made by Harry Colt in 1925, and by Eddie Hackett in the `60s.

COURSE INFORMATION & FACILITIES

Castlerock Golf Club
65 Circular Road, Castlerock,
Co. Londonderry. BT51 4TJ

Secretary: R. G. McBride
Tel: 01265 848314. Fax: 01265 849440.

Golf Professional: Robert Kelly
Tel: 01265 848314. Fax: 01265 849440.

Green Fees:
Weekdays – £25. Weekends – £35.
Weekdays (day) – £40. Weekends (day) – £50.
Handicap certificate required. Time restrictions apply.

CARD OF THE COURSE – PAR 72

1	2	3	4	5	6	7	8	9	Out
348	375	509	200	477	347	409	411	200	3276
Par 4	Par 4	Par 5	Par 3	Par 5	Par 4	Par 4	Par 4	Par 3	Par 36

10	11	12	13	14	15	16	17	18	In
391	509	430	379	192	518	157	493	342	3411
Par 4	Par 5	Par 4	Par 4	Par 3	Par 5	Par 3	Par 5	Par 4	Par 37

HOW TO GET THERE

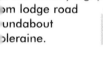

miles west of Coleraine, on
e A2. Clearly signposted
om lodge road
undabout
leraine.

Castlerock Golf Club

Connemara

Connemara is another of those Irish courses where you feel as if you're at the very edge of civilisation. Its hard to believe there is actually a golf course in this remote part of County Galway, yet here lies a fabulous links some five miles beyond the town of Clifden at Ballyconneely.

Eddie Hackett is responsible for Connemara. He built the course in 1973, taking full advantage of the huge rocks which characterise the landscape. In fact, Hackett was able to design the course without moving a single rock, a tribute to his skill as an architect. While this is a bona fide links, you won't find the type of sand dunes you would normally expect. This means you are more at the mercy of the winds that whip over the course from the Atlantic Ocean.

And, yes, there is always a wind.

Calm days at Connemara are rare indeed. You'll pray for such a day, however, when you look at the scorecard, for this is a very long golf course. Play it from the back if there is no wind or you're feeling brave, otherwise play from the forward tees. To give you an example, there are par fours of 475 yards (8th), 443 yards (9th), 432 yards (10th), 451 yards (12th) and 452 yards (16th), plus the four par fives measure 576 yards (7th), 523 yards (14th), 532 yards (17th) and 537 yards (18th). Be sure to make the most of the front nine, as it is about 300 yards shorter than the back nine.

Connemara provides superb views of the Atlantic Ocean, and of an imposing mountain range known locally as 'The Twelve Bens'.

COURSE INFORMATION & FACILITIES

Connemara Golf Club
Ballyconneely, Clifden
Co. Galway.

Secretary/Manager: John McLaughlin.
Tel: 095 2350. Fax: 095 23662.

Golf Professional: Hugh O'Neill.
Tel: 095 2350. Fax: 095 23662.

Green Fees:
May/June/July/Aug/Sept – IR£30.
April/Oct - IR£25.
Jan /Feb/March/Nov/Dec – IR£20.
Handicap certificate required. Society Outings (20 Minimum).

CARD OF THE COURSE (metres) – PAR 72

1	2	3	4	5	6	7	8	9	Out
349	385	154	358	360	193	531	438	408	3176
Par 4	Par 4	Par 3	Par 4	Par 4	Par 3	Par 5	Par 4	Par 4	Par 35
10	11	12	13	14	15	16	17	18	In
398	171	416	196	483	367	417	491	496	3435
Par 4	Par 3	Par 4	Par 3	Par 5	Par 4	Par 4	Par 5	Par 5	Par 37

HOW TO GET THERE

om Clifden, continue to
ıllyconneely where you will
rn right (straight on for
ɔundstone), then turn right
ɡain before the Pier, where
»u will find the golf club.

Connemara
Golf Club

County Louth

When a connoisseur of links golf arrives in Dublin he doesn't have to travel far to experience some of the finest seaside golf in Ireland. Immediately to the north of the capital are four outstanding links courses: Royal Dublin, Portmarnock, The Portmarnock Hotel Links and The Island. After playing these great courses it is difficult to avoid the temptation to zoom off to the magical west, and yet, less than an hour's drive north from Portmarnock there is a wonderful links situated just beyond the town of Drogheda.

Baltray is the place to head for – or more correctly, the County Louth Golf Club. This is unquestionably one of the top ten links courses in Ireland. It is a very natural-looking, quite understated layout. It is not particularly long, nor especially rugged, and the changes in elevation are more subtle than sweeping. Baltray was designed by Tom Simpson, which gives it a fine pedigree since he was also the principal architect of the Old Course at Ballybunion and Cruden Bay.

Simpson's artful routing maximised the effects of the wind and he incorporated great variety in hole length and direction. There is a superb quartet of par three holes, 'Baltray's four little gems', while the finest sequence comes between the 12th and 14th; it comprises two strong par fours and, quite possibly, the best drive-and-pitch par four in Ireland. And don't rush the tee shot on the 14th – the views are spectacular and on a clear day you can just see the fabled Mountains of Mourne.

HOW TO GET THERE

miles north east of town of
rogheda.

Co. Louth
Golf Club

COURSE INFORMATION & FACILITIES

 Co. Louth Golf Club
Baltray, Drogheda,
Co. Louth.

Secretary/Manager: Michael Delany.
Tel: 041 9822329. Fax: 041 9822969.

Golf Professional Paddy McGuire Tel: 041 9822444.

Green Fees:
Weekdays – IR£50. Weekends – IR£60.
Weekdays (day) – IR£50. Weekends (day) – IR£60.
Tuesdays all day and Wednesday afternoons (Ladies Day).

CARD OF THE COURSE – PAR 73

1	2	3	4	5	6	7	8	9	Out
433	482	544	344	158	531	163	407	419	3481
Par 4	Par 5	Par 5	Par 4	Par 3	Par 5	Par 3	Par 4	Par 4	Par 37

10	11	12	13	14	15	16	17	18	In
398	481	410	421	332	152	388	179	541	3302
Par 4	Par 5	Par 4	Par 4	Par 4	Par 3	Par 4	Par 3	Par 5	Par 36

County Sligo

*I*f you're going to play County Sligo, or Rosses Point as it's also known, then you might just want to consider brushing up on your knowledge of the verse of William Butler Yeats, Ireland's most famous poet.

The land around Sligo is Yeats' country. In fact he is buried nearby, within sight of Benbulben, the mountain that dominates the region and much of Yeats' poetry. You may not appreciate poetry, but rest assured that Rosses Point will have you waxing lyrical after just one round. This is a links course that has many fans; Tom Watson, Peter Alliss and Bernhard Langer – to name but a few – have all sung its praises.

There are many courses in Ireland with great views, and Rosses Point is no exception. From as early as the 3rd tee you are presented with stunning views of Drumcliffe Bay, the Atlantic Ocean, the Ox Mountains and Benbulben, Yeats' mountain. Enjoy the views on the 3rd, for after a bunkerless, medium iron par three, the real test that is County Sligo begins at the 5th. This hole is called 'the Jump' and is aptly named as you jump from the high ground around the clubhouse down into real golfing country. This par five hole calls for a shot to be played from a clifftop tee to a fairway lying far below you. This is true links land, amidst sand dunes, pot bunkers and elusive undulating greens.

County Sligo is the venue for the West of Ireland Championship, a prestigious amateur event with many fine winners dating back to 1924. Oh, and Harry Colt had a hand in the design of the course – that should be enough to whet your appetite to visit Sligo Town.

HOW TO GET THERE

km north west of Sligo town
Rosses Point village.

County Sligo
Golf Club

COURSE INFORMATION & FACILITIES

County Sligo Golf Club
Rosses Point,
Co. Sligo.

Acting Administration Manager: Teresa Banks.
Tel: 071 77134/77186. Fax: 071 77460.

Golf Professional: Leslie Roberson. Tel: 071 77171.

Green Fees:
Weekdays – IR£32. Weekends – IR£40.
Letter of introduction and Handicap certificate required.

CARD OF THE COURSE (metres) – PAR 71

1	2	3	4	5	6	7	8	9	Out
347	278	457	150	438	379	393	374	153	2969
Par 4	Par 4	Par 5	Par 3	Par 5	Par 4	Par 4	Par 4	Par 3	Par 36

10	11	12	13	14	15	16	17	18	In
351	368	486	162	394	367	196	414	336	3074
Par 4	Par 4	Par 5	Par 3	Par 4	Par 4	Par 3	Par 4	Par 4	Par 35

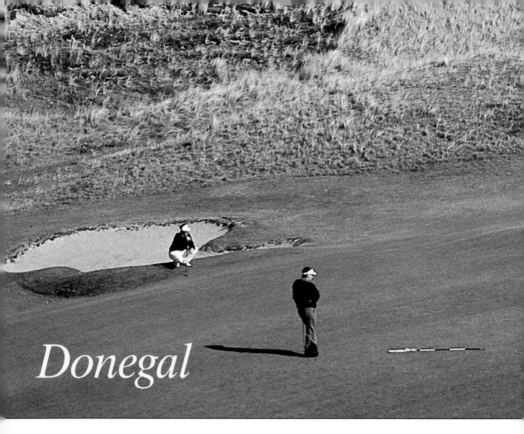

Donegal

"*D*on't go to Donegal and miss Murvagh." Those were the words of Christy O'Connor Jnr. Now when a famous Irish golfer gives you a tip, it pays to listen. Donegal, often called Murvagh is a true hidden gem. Play it and you'll be convinced it's been there for at least a hundred years. It hasn't – this superb links course was laid down in 1973. The ubiquitous Eddie Hackett created a challenge that will test the best, for the course measures over 7,150 yards.

The opening four holes don't really give you a taste of what's to come. Although they're good, they are played over land that can't really be called true links. Starting at the 5th you are into links country proper, in amongst the dunes. The hole is a beauty, too, a par three of 187 yards with a stage-like green. To come up short is to roll back into a nest of bunkers, from where par is virtually impossible.

Murvagh is a man-sized golf course; coming home you face one of the longest par fives in Ireland. The 12th hole measures almost 600 yards and calls for three full wood shots from most mortals. Then there's the 16th, which is a par three of 240 yards.

Play Murvagh from sensible tees unless you've got some sort of masochistic streak in you. And enjoy the fine views the course offers of the Atlantic and the mountains of Donegal – they'll more than compensate for the troubles you'll be experiencing if you do attempt to play from the back markers. But Christy's right – don't miss Murvagh!

HOW TO GET THERE

ff the N15, main
onegal/Ballyshannon road. 8
les South of Donegal Town.
miles North of Ballyshannon.

Donegal
Golf Links

COURSE INFORMATION & FACILITIES

Donegal Golf Club
Murvagh, Laghey,
Co. Donegal.

Administrator: John Mcbride.
Tel: 073 34054. Fax: 073 34377.

Green Fees:
Weekdays – IR£20. Weekends – IR£27.
Weekdays (day) – IR£20. Weekends (day) – IR£40.
Handicap Certificate required. Some time restrictions.
Advance bookings necessary.

CARD OF THE COURSE (metres) – PAR 73

1	2	3	4	5	6	7	8	9	Out
485	423	193	441	172	469	391	502	368	3444
Par 5	Par 4	Par 3	Par 4	Par 3	Par 5	Par 4	Par 5	Par 4	Par 37

10	11	12	13	14	15	16	17	18	In
322	371	543	147	510	367	222	325	368	3175
Par 4	Par 4	Par 5	Par 3	Par 5	Par 4	Par 3	Par 4	Par 4	Par 36

Enniscrone

*E*nniscrone is set to do a Portstewart. It is about to open six new holes which, when incorporated into the present layout, should establish Enniscrone as one of the very finest links in Ireland. Not that it isn't close already.

Situated at the point where County Sligo meets County Mayo, and somewhat wedged between the Ox Mountains and Killala Bay (a fisherman's paradise), Enniscrone enjoys a glorious setting; the links itself overlooks a vast pristine white beach.

The golf course was originally laid out by Eddie Hackett. It possesses many strong and characterful holes, its only weakness being the first few holes – particularly the 1st and 2nd which are both fairly

pedestrian par fives. They will not be part of the 'championship 18' when the new holes are ready for play (in 2001), rather they will be included in a newly created 'third nine.' As at Portstewart, the six new holes have been carved out of adjacent dramatic duneland. Enniscrone will become one of those rare links courses that golfers with high blood pressure should avoid playing.

In the current layout the most celebrated holes are the 9th and 10th – the former with its huge amphitheatre green, and the latter with its exhilarating downhill drive and rollercoasting fairway. Yes, they are classic links holes, and ones that provide a foretaste of what's to come when Enniscrone joins golf's premier league.

COURSE INFORMATION & FACILITIES

Enniscrone Golf Links
Enniscrone,
Co. Sligo.

Administrator: Anne Freeman.
Tel: 096 36297. Fax: 096 36657.

Golf Professional Charlie Mc Goldrick
Tel: 096 36666. Fax: 096 36657

Green Fees:
Weekdays – IR£25. Weekends: IR£34.
Weekdays (day) – IR£40.
Some time restrictions.

CARD OF THE COURSE – PAR 72

1	2	3	4	5	6	7	8	9	Out
551	535	395	534	170	395	374	170	345	3469
Par 5	Par 5	Par 4	Par 5	Par 3	Par 4	Par 4	Par 3	Par 4	Par 37

10	11	12	13	14	15	16	17	18	In
350	427	540	202	368	412	403	149	400	3251
Par 4	Par 4	Par 5	Par 3	Par 4	Par 4	Par 4	Par 3	Par 4	Par 35

HOW TO GET THERE

Off R297 Enniscrone/Ballina
Road, 13km Ballina Town.
36km Knock airport.
45km Sligo airport.

Enniscrone
Golf Links

Lahinch

Two legendary figures shaped the golf course at Lahinch: Old Tom Morris, arguably the greatest golf architect of the 19th century; and Alister Mackenzie, arguably the greatest golf architect of the 20th century. Given that Old Tom was initially responsible for, among others, Royal County Down, Prestwick and Royal Dornoch, and that Mackenzie created Augusta, Cypress Point and Royal Melbourne, it is hardly surprising that between them they crafted an extraordinary links.

Lahinch is known as 'the St Andrews of Ireland' – not because of the association with Old Tom, but because the Lahinch community lives and breathes golf. It is situated on the coast of County Clare, a short drive from the dramatic Cliffs of Moher. Any golfer making the pilgrimage to Ballybunion

should visit Lahinch if nowhere else.

The Old Course (for there are now 36 holes) has been described as a cross between Ballybunion and Prestwick. The dunes at Lahinch are not as extensive as those at Ballybunion, although in places they are just as impressive. Midway through a round, between the 7th and the 12th, golfers play a sequence of holes that are every bit as thrilling as the back nine at Ballybunion.

Old Tom's influence and the similarities with Prestwick are most evident at the 5th and 6th, both of which feature blind shots. Not too many people raise eyebrows at the 5th as it's a par five, but the following hole is a par three!

Commentators are occasionally critical of Lahinch's finish, suggesting that it's an anti-climax. Nonsense! Lahinch charms and challenges from first to last.

HOW TO GET THERE

...om the town of Ennis, take
... N67 to Ennistymon and
...inch is two miles from
...nistymon
... the sea.
...s well
...nposted.

Lahinch
Golf Club

COURSE INFORMATION & FACILITIES

Lahinch Golf Club
Lahinch,
Co. Clare.

Secretary/Manager: Alan Reardon.
Tel: 065 7081003. Fax: 065 7081592.

Golf Professional:
Tel: 065 7081408 Fax: 065 7081592.

Green Fees (old course):
Weekdays – IR£50. Weekends – IR£50.
Weekdays (day) – IR£50. Weekends (day) – IR£50.

Letter of introduction and handicap certificate required.
Some time restrictions.

CARD OF THE COURSE (Old Course) – PAR 72

1	2	3	4	5	6	7	8	9	Out
385	512	151	428	482	155	399	350	384	3246
Par 4	Par 5	Par 3	Par 4	Par 5	Par 3	Par 4	Par 4	Par 4	Par 36

10	11	12	13	14	15	16	17	18	In
451	138	475	273	488	462	195	437	533	3452
Par 4	Par 3	Par 4	Par 4	Par 5	Par 4	Par 3	Par 4	Par 5	Par 36

Portmarnock

*P*ortmarnock is Ireland's premier championship venue. In addition to hosting numerous Irish Opens, the links has staged the World Cup (in 1960) and the Walker Cup (in 1991) – American teams winning on both occasions. Somewhat surprisingly it has also been the venue for a British Amateur Championship and, somewhat ridiculously, it has never hosted the Ryder Cup.

Portmarnock is a magnificent links. Located just a few miles north of Dublin, it occupies a peninsula and is effectively surrounded by water on three sides. Being so exposed, the player is often at the mercy of the elements; indeed, Portmarnock can pose as tough a challenge as any links in the world.

From its championship tees the course measures in excess of 7100 yards. The links is

both expertly and heavily bunkered and the rough really is rough. But Portmarnock, rather like Muirfield, is regarded as a very 'fair' links. There is, for instance, only one blind tee shot (at the 5th); the fairways do not undulate significantly, thus awkward stances are the product of poor golf not poor fortune, and as the course is arranged in two loops of nine there is a great sense of balance.

Perhaps the finest sequence at Portmarnock occurs between the 4th and the 8th, although the best and possibly most difficult hole of all is the par three 15th. It is played parallel to the shore and if the wind is whipping in off the Irish Sea you have to start your tee shot out over the beach! Ben Crenshaw has called the 15th, 'one of the greatest short holes on Earth.'

COURSE INFORMATION & FACILITIES

Portmarnock Golf Club
Portmarnock,
Co. Dublin.

Secretary/Manager: John Quigley.
Tel: 01 8462968. Fax: 01 8462601.
Golf Professional: Tel: 01 8462634.
Green Fees:
Weekdays – IR£75. Weekends – IR£95.
Letter of introduction and handicap certificate required.
Some time restrictions.

CARD OF THE COURSE (metres) – PAR 72

1	2	3	4	5	6	7	8	9	Out
355	346	351	403	364	550	168	364	399	3300
Par 4	Par 4	Par 4	Par 4	Par 4	Par 5	Par 3	Par 4	Par 4	Par 36

10	11	12	13	14	15	16	17	18	In
341	392	139	516	350	173	480	429	377	3197
Par 4	Par 4	Par 3	Par 5	Par 4	Par 3	Par 5	Par 4	Par 4	Par 36

HOW TO GET THERE

low M50 to Malahide and
to Portmarnock by the
ıst road.

Portmarnock Hotel Links

*T*he Portmarnock Hotel & Golf Links lies adjacent to Portmarnock Golf Club. The hotel, once the home of the Jameson (whiskey) family, became fully operational in June 1996. The new links was designed by Bernhard Langer, a three-time winner of the Irish Open, and the architect was Stan Eby. Together they have produced a masterpiece.

Perhaps the most immediately striking aspect of the links is how natural it appears. There is nothing flamboyant about the design, and it is refreshing to see that no fewer than five of the par fours measure less than 380 yards. The course flows, almost gracefully, from green to tee to green. As at St Andrews and Ballybunion Old Course, there are no lengthy walks in between holes.

The other very obvious feature is the quality and extent of the bunkering. There are almost 100 bunkers in total and each has been painstakingly and skilfully constructed with steep revetted faces, similar to Carnoustie and Muirfield. In fact, the Portmarnock Hotel links bears more of a resemblance generally to those two great Scottish courses than to neighbouring Portmarnock. More specifically, the front nine is reminiscent of Carnoustie and the back nine of Muirfield, although it could be argued that the four final holes are more thrilling than those at either of the Scottish links.

In true Carnoustie style, then, the opening few holes demand a 'keep your head down' approach. The views are hardly distracting, but the challenge is very evident. The landscape becomes more appealing from the 8th hole onwards. Aside from the climactic finish, the 8th is possibly the finest hole on the course. The fairway dog-legs sharply to the left before tumbling in classic links fashion towards a severely sloping green perched amid some very wild-looking dunes. The great finish begins at the 15th, where the approach must somehow be threaded past (or over) a sea of deep traps. The 16th is played from a superbly elevated tee. The 17th is yet another formidable short hole – beware the very cavernous greenside bunker – and the 18th descends from a lofty tee to an amphitheatre green surrounded by towering sand dunes and devilish pot bunkers. The perfect stage for a winning birdie!

COURSE INFORMATION & FACILITIES

Portmarnock Hotel & Golf Links
Portmarnock,
Co. Dublin.

Director of Golf: Moira Cassidy
Tel: 01-846-1800. Fax: 01-846-1077.

Green Fees:
Non – Hotel Residents IR£60
Hotel Residents IR£38

CARD OF THE COURSE (metres) – PAR 71

1	2	3	4	5	6	7	8	9	Out
304	305	172	512	409	462	405	323	139	3031
Par 4	Par 4	Par 3	Par 5	Par 4	Par 5	Par 4	Par 4	Par 3	Par 36

10	11	12	13	14	15	16	17	18	In
467	406	316	135	312	345	354	171	365	2878
Par 5	Par 4	Par 4	Par 3	Par 4	Par 4	Par 4	Par 3	Par 4	Par 35

HOW TO GET THERE

From Dublin Airport turn left
t first roundabout, Belfast
oad – take inside lane, exit
ght to Malahide, look out
r signs Portmarnock Hotel
Golf Links, 1½ miles turn
ft at lights.

Portstewart

*U*ntil quite recent times Portstewart was widely regarded as 'a good links with an exceptional opening hole.' Rather like Machrihanish on Scotland's Mull of Kintyre (which as the crow flies is no great distance), Portstewart's remaining holes were somewhat overlooked on account of the astonishing start.

Nowadays, Portstewart is viewed in a very different light – the 'exceptional' tag is not limited to the 1st hole. The reason for the seachange in perception can be summarised in two words: 'Thistly Hollow.'

Until the late 1980s golfers would play the famous 1st (a left to right dog-leg that features a dramatic downhill tee shot), then gaze up into the vast range of sandhills known as

Thistly Hollow behind the 1st green and contemplate how amazing it would be if only the club could build some holes in amongst those dunes. Well, it happened! Seven new holes were constructed and the result is that Portstewart can now boast one of the finest front nines in golf. The pick of these 'new' holes may be the 3rd, a strong par three that might have been plucked from Royal Birkdale; the beautifully flowing par five 4th; the heroic two-shot 5th, and the 'Postage Stamp' like 6th.

Portstewart is situated only a few miles west of Portrush, and to the west of Portstewart is Castlerock. Together they make a superb trio; throw in the spectacular scenery of the Giant's Causeway Coast and you have a magnificent golfing destination.

COURSE INFORMATION & FACILITIES

Portstewart Golf Club
Strand Head, Portstewart.
Co Londonderry

Manager: Michael Moss.
Tel: 01265 833839. Fax: 01265 834097.

Golf Professional Alan Hunter Tel/Fax: 01265 832601.

Green Fees:
Weekdays – £45. Weekends – £65.
Weekdays (day) – £65.
Letter of introduction and handicap certificate required.
Time restrictions apply.

CARD OF THE COURSE – PAR 72

1	2	3	4	5	6	7	8	9	Out
425	366	207	535	456	140	511	384	352	3376
Par 4	Par 4	Par 3	Par 5	Par 4	Par 3	Par 5	Par 4	Par 4	Par 36

10	11	12	13	14	15	16	17	18	In
393	370	166	500	485	169	422	434	464	3403
Par 4	Par 4	Par 3	Par 5	Par 5	Par 3	Par 4	Par 4	Par 4	Par 36

HOW TO GET THERE

llow signs for Portstewart –
ce there follow signs for
and Beach. Golf Club is
:ated on left overlooking
e beach.

Portstewart
Golf Club

O'Malley's
Edgewater
Hotel
Portstewart

This 28 ensuite bedroom hotel, situated overlooking the Strand at Portstewart with outstanding views of the Hills of Donegal and the Atlantic Ocean provides an ideal base for your golfing holiday with the North Coast's top courses within easy reach.

Special midweek and weekend breaks available throughout the year

Dine overlooking the Atlantic with bar snacks served throughout the day in the Inishtrahull Lounge (12.30-9.00pm) and the Restaurant every evening from 7pm offering a wide range of dishes from our extensive A La Carte Menu.

The following courses are within easy reach of the hotel:

Portstewart - three minutes walk; **Royal Portrush** - two courses (one championship links) four miles; **Castlerock, Ballycastle, Bushfoot** - (nine holes).

For further information and reservations
Tel: 028 70 833314 Fax: 028 70 832224
email:edgewater.hotel@virgin.net or visit our
website:http://freespace.virgin.net/edgewater.hotel/index.htm

88 Strand Road, Portstewart, Co L'Derry. BT55 7LZ

Rosslare

For many overseas visitors Rosslare is the gateway to Ireland. Situated not far from the busy ferry port is Rosslare golf links, and stories abound of touring golfers who have dropped in on the course, played 18 holes, and then never ventured beyond Rosslare for the remainder of their trip - the links is that good! Yet you rarely see Rosslare ranked among the top 30 or 40 courses in Ireland, which it surely deserves to be. The club is old enough and established enough but presumably it gets overlooked by critics because the links is forever being tinkered with, the layout forever being revised or refined.

Rosslare is 'The Island of the South East': a splendidly old fashioned links with some magnificent duneland terrain. The fairways twist and tumble in a manner very reminiscent of the north Dublin course. True, some holes are a little quirky, a little too blind for the purists, but Rosslare has enormous character. There are also some magnificent views - the course starts and finishes under a canopy of beautiful sea pines and almost half the holes are played very close to the sea.

Some solid hitting is required to master Rosslare's exacting finishing stretch, from the 15th onwards, but the most interesting sequence comes between the 4th and the 7th, and the last of these, a superb rollercoasting par five, is the best on the course. Other note-worthy holes are the 11th, 13th and 14th, all of which exude charm - a quality Rosslare has in abundance.

COURSE INFORMATION & FACILITIES

Rosslare Golf Links
Rosslare Strand
Co. Wexford

Secretary: James F Hall
Tel: 00353 53 32203. Fax: 00353 53 32263

Golf Professional: 00353 53 32238

Green Fees:
Weekdays – IR£25. Weekends – IR£35.
Weekdays (day) – IR£25. Weekends (day) – IR£35.

Please ring for bookings. Tuesday – Ladies Day.

CARD OF THE COURSE – PAR 72

1	2	3	4	5	6	7	8	9	Out
382	194	542	373	443	335	554	177	414	3414
Par 4	Par 3	Par 5	Par 4	Par 3	Par 4	Par 5	Par 3	Par 4	Par 36

10	11	12	13	14	15	16	17	18	In
167	481	494	282	172	403	400	420	482	3301
Par 3	Par 4	Par 5	Par 4	Par 3	Par 4	Par 4	Par 4	Par 5	Par 36

HOW TO GET THERE

miles from ferry terminal at
osslare Harbour, 10 miles
outh of Wexford town.

Royal County Down

Bernard Darwin once summarised the appeal of Royal County Down by suggesting that it offered, 'the kind of golf that people play in their most ecstatic dreams.' Another celebrated English writer, Peter Dobereiner, described the Newcastle links as, 'exhilarating even without a club in your hand.' At one time or another Royal County Down has been adjudged more beautiful than Turnberry, more spectacular than Ballybunion, more natural than Royal Dornoch and more punishing than Carnoustie.

More beautiful than Turnberry and more spectacular than Ballybunion? Newcastle is where, in the immortal words of Percy French, 'the Mountains of Mourne sweep down to the sea.' Fringed by the impressive sweep of Dundrum Bay, towering sandhills appear wrapped in bright yellow gorse during spring, and in autumn are liberally sprinkled with purple heather. The views from the 4th tee and the crest of the 9th fairway are quite mesmerising, while the 2nd, 3rd, 4th, 8th, 9th, 13th, 15th and 16th could all be described as sensational holes.

More natural than Royal Dornoch? Old Tom Morris (ably assisted by Mother Nature) was the original architect of both Newcastle and Dornoch. With its plethora of blind tee shots, Newcastle is the more old fashioned layout. The contours of its fairways and greens appear completely untouched by man – and surely no one could have created those wild, tussocky-faced bunkers!

And more punishing than Carnoustie? The greens at Newcastle are invariably smaller, the rough is more severe and Carnoustie's bunkers appear tame by comparison.

The most beautiful, most spectacular, most natural and most difficult links … Surely, there is none finer?

HOW TO GET THERE

ewcastle is 30 miles south
f Belfast via the A24; 90
iles north of Dublin via the
1 to Newry, and 25 miles
ast of Newry via the
25.

COURSE INFORMATION & FACILITIES

Royal County Down
36 Golf Links Road, Newcastle,
Co. Down.

Secretary: Peter Rolph.
Tel: 028 43723314. Fax: 028 43726281.
e-mail: royal.co.down@virgin.net

Golf Professional Kevan J. Whitson Tel: 028 43722419.

Green Fees:
Weekdays – £70. Weekends – £80.
Letter of introduction and handicap certificate required.
Some time restrictions. Visitors Mon/Tue/Thu/Fri.

CARD OF THE COURSE – PAR 71

1	2	3	4	5	6	7	8	9	Out
506	421	474	212	438	396	145	429	486	3507
Par 5	Par 4	Par 4	Par 3	Par 4	Par 4	Par 3	Par 4	Par 5	Par 36

10	11	12	13	14	15	16	17	18	In
197	438	525	443	213	464	276	427	547	3530
Par 3	Par 4	Par 5	Par 4	Par 3	Par 4	Par 4	Par 4	Par 5	Par 36

Royal Dublin

R oyal Dublin may be the closest thing in Ireland to the Old Course at St Andrews. Laid out over a narrow tract of land, it is the only one of Ireland's great links that stretches out and back in traditional 'Scotttish' style. Like St Andrews the land is essentially flat with subtle undulations. Wind and pin position dictate a player's strategy, the greens are kept firm and fast, and bump and run is king.

The golf club dates from 1885. Initially 'home' was a confined area in Phoenix Park, but in 1889 the club moved to its present site at Bull Island, still within the city limits. Bull Island is accessed by a wooden bridge and the duneland terrain is shared by golfers, bird watchers and botanists. It is an extraordinary domain.

A combination of greater length and the prevailing wind ensures that the inward nine is invariably the tougher half. However, the outward nine includes arguably the two best holes, namely the par four 5th and the par five 8th. The inward nine starts to bare its teeth at the 13th. This is a formidable two-shotter where the entrance to the green is cambered and very narrow – rather appropriately the hole is called 'Dardanelles'.

The most famous hole at Royal Dublin is the 18th, 'Garden', a right-angled par four. The approach must be fired directly over an Out of Bounds field (the eponymous garden) to reach the green in two. Royal Dublin has staged many important championships over the years and the closing hole has provided many dramatic finishes.

COURSE INFORMATION & FACILITIES

Royal Dublin Golf Club
North Bull Island, Dollymount,
Dublin 3.

Secretary/Manager: John Lambe.
Tel: 353 (0)1 8336346. Fax: 353 (0)1 8336504.

Golf Professional Leonard Owens
Tel:353 (0)1 8336477. Fax:353 (0)1 8531795

Green Fees:
Weekdays – IR£60. Weekends – IR£70.
Weekdays (day) – IR£90.
Handicap certificate required. Some time restrictions.

CARD OF THE COURSE (metres) – PAR 72

1	2	3	4	5	6	7	8	9	Out
361	445	363	163	423	180	322	440	164	2902
Par 4	Par 5	Par 4	Par 3	Par 4	Par 3	Par 4	Par 5	Par 3	Par 35
10	11	12	13	14	15	16	17	18	In
374	483	172	381	439	390	241	341	430	3251
Par 4	Par 5	Par 3	Par 4	Par 5	Par 4	Par 4	Par 4	Par 4	Par 37

HOW TO GET THERE

al Dublin is on an island
niles from the centre of
blin City. It is reached by a
oden bridge off the main
th Dublin Bay road.

al Dublin
olf Club

White Sands
HOTEL

*Set in Idyllic Portmarnock, White Sands Hotel offers tranquil
surroundings amidst fresh air and still remains within easy reach of
Dublin City & Dublin Airport. Conveniently located to all major golf
courses including Royal Dublin, Malahide Golf Club and
Portmarnock Golf Links.*

*All 32 bedrooms are ensuite offering modern amenities, some with
spectacular sea views.*

*The Hotel's facilities comprise of Function and Conference Rooms,
The Oasis Bar, The Kingdford Smith Restaurant serving
contemporary food with Irish flair and the renowned Tamango
Nightclub. The perfect venue for all your requirements.*

COAST ROAD, PORTMARNOCK, CO. DUBLIN, IRELAND.
TEL: +353 (0)1 8460003   FAX: +353 (0)1 8460420
EMAIL: SANDSHOTEL@TINET.IE

Royal Portrush

*I*t is remarkable that a country as small as Northern Ireland should have two of the Top 12 Golf Courses in the World. But, in Royal County Down and Royal Portrush, and according to America's two biggest selling golf publications, it has precisely that. Arguments as to which is the better of the two links have raged for more than a century.

There are 36 holes at Portrush with the Dunluce and the Valley Courses, the former being the one on which the 1951 (British) Open Championship was staged.

Portrush was shaped by master architect Harry Colt. There are many who regard the Dunluce Course as Colt's finest achievement – notwithstanding that he was also responsible for Muirfield. As for Portrush's setting, let's just say that among the courses presently on the Open Championship rota, only Turnberry's scenery can compare. Portrush is situated on the Antrim coast, close to the Giant's Causeway, and even closer to Dunluce Castle from which the championship links takes its name. The most striking view of the links is to be gained from the main coast road that approaches Portrush from the east.

The front nine of the Dunluce is particularly outstanding. The most famous hole is undoubtedly the 5th, 'White Rocks', a shortish par four that charges downhill from spectacular tee to a green perched on the edge of the links, overlooking the sea. The 14th 'Calamity' often provides the defining moment of the back nine. It is a real 'death or glory' hole – a 210 yards par three with a tee shot across the edge of an enormous ravine.

COURSE INFORMATION & FACILITIES

Royal Portrush Golf Club
Dunluce Road, Portrush,
Co. Antrim.

Secretary/Manager: Wilma Erskine.
Tel: 01265 822311. Fax: 01265 823139.

Golf Professional Dai Stevenson Tel: 01265-823335.

Green Fees:
Weekdays – £50. Weekends – £60. (per round)
Letter of introduction and handicap certificate required.
Some time restrictions

CARD OF THE COURSE – PAR 72

1	2	3	4	5	6	7	8	9	Out
392	505	155	457	384	189	431	384	475	3372
Par 4	Par 5	Par 3	Par 4	Par 4	Par 3	Par 4	Par 4	Par 5	Par 36

10	11	12	13	14	15	16	17	18	In
478	170	392	386	210	365	428	548	469	3446
Par 5	Par 3	Par 4	Par 4	Par 3	Par 4	Par 4	Par 5	Par 4	Par 36

HOW TO GET THERE

om Belfast take M2 North,
rn on to A26, follow to
rtrush. Links can be seen
you enter town.

The European Club

*I*t is the proud boast of golfers at Mount Juliet that they play 'the course that Jack built.' Near Brittas Bay in County Wicklow we can now experience the links that Pat built. Whatever else Pat Ruddy achieves in his life, The European Club will stand as his monument to golf.

The word 'great' should be used very sparingly in relation to golf courses, but the links at Brittas Bay which opened as recently as 1993 is undoubtedly a great links. It has many great qualities. The sandhills are not quite of Ballybunion-like proportion, but they dwarf those at Portmarnock. Better still, the golf course never leaves the dunes. There is balance and consistency and no feeling of mild disappointment, as is sometimes expressed in relation to the final few holes at Lahinch and Newcastle – and indeed with regard to the first few at Portmarnock and Ballybunion.

The Irish Sea is the golfer's constant companion. You see it as you leave the 1st green, you hear it as you approach the 3rd and smell it as you stroll down the 7th – and you can almost touch it as you play along the 12th and 13th.

There are at least six genuinely great holes at The European Club: the beautifully flowing downhill 3rd, the 7th with its fairway bordered by haunting marshland, the 8th, the 11th, the 12th and the fabulous 17th which plunges through a secluded dune-lined valley.

One final treat – or is it a shock – awaits at the 18th. But who are we to spoil the surprise?

COURSE INFORMATION & FACILITIES

The European Club
Brittas Bay,
Co. Wicklow.

Secretary: Sidon Ruddy.
Tel: 0404 47415. Fax: 0404 47449.

Green Fees:
Weekdays – IR£50. Weekends – IR£50.
Weekdays (day) – IR£70. Weekends (day) – IR£70.

CARD OF THE COURSE – PAR 71

1	2	3	4	5	6	7	8	9	Out
392	160	499	452	409	187	470	415	427	3411
Par 4	Par 3	Par 5	Par 4	Par 4	Par 3	Par 4	Par 4	Par 4	Par 35

10	11	12	13	14	15	16	17	18	In
417	389	459	596	165	401	415	391	445	3678
Par 4	Par 4	Par 4	Par 5	Par 3	Par 4	Par 4	Par 4	Par 4	Par 36

HOW TO GET THERE

11 South 30 miles from
central Dublin. At Jack White's
n, turn left into Brittas Bay.
T junction at Beach, turn
ht & go 1.5 miles to Links.

The Island

Although founded over a century ago, The Island Golf Club near Malahide is one of Ireland's greatest golfing secrets. There are several reasons for this, chief of which is the links' close proximity to Royal Dublin and Portmarnock, two very well established championship venues. Another is that until quite recently the principal mode of transport to The Island was by ferry.

In fact it isn't literally an island – the course occupies a peninsula, directly across the estuary from Malahide. The rather eccentric voyage discouraged many but for those with a spirit of adventure it merely added to the allure and charm of the links.

The Island enjoys some of the most naturally rugged terrain on the east coast.

It has been called 'the Lahinch of the east' and the sandhills dwarf those at Portmarnock. When the course was originally laid out (it is not clear by whom) little attempt was made to tame the landscape and the links was built right in amongst the dunes.

Although changes have occurred over the years (the ferry was discontinued in 1973 when a newly sited clubhouse opened) the course has kept its essential character. In 1990, the club's centenary year, a revised layout was unveiled. It included several new holes but also retained the best of the old layout, including the wonderful sequence between the 12th and the 15th, which tour the tip of the peninsula.

HOW TO GET THERE

ke the main Dublin/Belfast
ad. 3 miles past Swords
ke the road to
nabate/Portrane, and
low signs to The
and Golf Club.

COURSE INFORMATION & FACILITIES

 The Island Golf Club
Corballis, Donabate,
Co. Dublin.

Golf Professional Kevin Kelliher Tel: 8435002.

Green Fees:
Weekdays – IR£50. Weekends – IR£60.

CARD OF THE COURSE (metres) – PAR 71

1	2	3	4	5	6	7	8	9	Out
396	363	405	320	336	300	403	282	159	2964
Par 4	Par 4	Par 4	Par 4	Par 4	Par 4	Par 4	Par 4	Par 3	Par 35

10	11	12	13	14	15	16	17	18	In
500	284	379	191	315	507	140	388	410	3114
Par 5	Par 4	Par 4	Par 3	Par 4	Par 5	Par 3	Par 4	Par 4	Par 36

Tralee

*I*f you've seen the film, *'Ryan's Daughter'*, then you probably know that Tralee possesses one of the world's most glorious beaches, not to mention scenery that is unrivalled anywhere in Ireland. The scenery hits you in all its glory from the moment you get to the first green and second tee. The vista is simply breathtaking and it is one that will enchant you for the rest of your round.

Arnold Palmer and Ed Seay are responsible for the layout at Tralee. Palmer had always wanted to create an Irish links course and was given the opportunity to do so in the early 1980s. Like the scenery, there are some holes that will take your breath away. The 2nd, for example, is a par five that runs along the clifftop, with a green placed perilously close to the edge – hit a wayward shot and it will land on the rocks far below! The 3rd hole is reminiscent of the 7th at Pebble Beach (albeit a longer version), where a shot is played to a green with the Atlantic Ocean dominating the backdrop. On the back nine you will no doubt find the par four 12th one of the most demanding two-shots in golf. At 434 yards it calls for a good drive followed by an extremely testing approach that must be played over a ravine to a plateau green. Make four here and you'll feel like you've birdied the hole. On the 13th you have to carry your shot over a deep chasm to find the putting surface – mercifully, it's only a 150 yard par three, but the bad news is that some days you have to hit a wood into the wind.

Still, if your round doesn't go quite to plan you can always admire the scenery!

COURSE INFORMATION & FACILITIES

Tralee Golf Club
West Barrow, Ardfert, Tralee,
Co. Kerry.

Club Supervisor: Michael O'Brien.
Tel: 066 36379. Fax: 066 36008.

Golf Professional: David Power.
Tel: 066 36379. Fax: 066 36008.

Green Fees:
Weekdays - £60, Weekends - £60. Not on Sunday
Handicap certificate required.

CARD OF THE COURSE (metres) – PAR 71

1	2	3	4	5	6	7	8	9	Out
368	542	183	388	391	389	143	354	451	3209
Par 4	Par 5	Par 3	Par 4	Par 4	Par 4	Par 3	Par 4	Par 5	Par 36

10	11	12	13	14	15	16	17	18	In
385	530	417	145	367	273	181	323	422	3043
Par 4	Par 5	Par 4	Par 3	Par 4	Par 4	Par 3	Par 4	Par 4	Par 35

HOW TO GET THERE

om Tralee, take the road to
dfert. After 11 km, take the
ft turn to Spa/Fenit. After
km, take the right turn to
rrow Harbour and after the
idge take the left fork.

167

Waterville

Jack Mulcahy was an Irish born American who, after making millions in the chemical business, sought a reason to return to Ireland. That reason became a golf course on the remote west coast of County Kerry at Waterville.

Eddie Hackett was the man Mulcahy entrusted to create one of the finest links in golf. Built in 1973, it didn't take long for Waterville's reputation to grow. Now it's on the itinerary of every visiting American golfer.

Waterville starts slowly with the first and second holes being slightly inland, but by the time you get to the 3rd tee you're in for a treat. This hole is a slicer's nightmare, with the Atlantic Ocean hugging the entire right-hand side of the fairway. But it is on the back nine that Waterville lives up to its premier billing. The 11th and 12th, for example, are links holes that would grace any great seaside course. The 11th is a par five called 'Tranquillity' and is played along a roller-coaster fairway through an avenue of tall dunes. It is one of the best par fives in golf. The 12th is called 'the Mass' hole because priests used to say Mass in a large hollow immediately below the green during a time in Irish history when Catholicism was outlawed. You won't find priests today, but you may just pray that your ball reaches the plateau green.

Without doubt, the best view of the course is provided by Mulcahy's Peak, which is the teeing area for the superb par three 17th. Sit here for as long as you possibly can without holding up the group behind. The panorama is stunning.

HOW TO GET THERE

ituated half way on the Ring
f Kerry. ¹/₄ mile off the main
ng of Kerry Road, on the
ast.

COURSE INFORMATION & FACILITIES

Waterville Golf Links
Waterville,
Co. Kerry.

Manager: Noel Cronin.
Tel: 066-74102. Fax: 066-74482.

Golf Professional Liam Higgins Tel: 066-74102.

Green Fees:
Weekdays – IR£60. Weekends – IR£60.
Weekdays (round) – IR£60. Weekends (round) – IR£60.
Letter of introduction and handicap certificate required.
Some time restrictions.

CARD OF THE COURSE – PAR 72

1	2	3	4	5	6	7	8	9	Out
430	469	417	179	595	371	178	435	445	3519
Par 4	Par 4	Par 4	Par 3	Par 5	Par 4	Par 3	Par 4	Par 4	Par 35

10	11	12	13	14	15	16	17	18	In
475	496	200	518	456	392	350	196	582	3665
Par 4	Par 5	Par 3	Par 5	Par 4	Par 4	Par 4	Par 3	Par 5	Par 37

INDEX

Experience LINKS®
Absolutely Free

MANY GOLFERS have discovered a different golf magazine than the ones that offer instruction. Hence the growing popularity of LINKS—The Best of Golf, which is in a class by itself.

The editors of LINKS bring the spirit of golf to life. The award-winning articles escort you down the fairways of the world's classic courses. You'll become an expert on the game's history and traditions. The previews of the majors are simply the best. Legendary golf commentators Jack Whitaker and Ben Wright provide insightful analysis; while Nick Faldo, with six major championships under his belt, writes a regular column as Playing Architecture Editor.

Above all, you'll see stunning photography throughout every issue. The entire publication exudes quality and impeccable taste. Seven times a year for the past 13 years, a group of dedicated employees has published LINKS. You will get a great deal of satisfaction from reading LINKS—The Best of Golf.

You cannot appreciate this fine title from a single issue, so the publisher has arranged for you to receive six months of LINKS—The Best of Golf absolutely free!

To receive your free six months (four issues), simply e-mail your name and address to: valb@linksmagazine.com

Spoilt for c*

From Britain's leading
golf book publisher, the
complete guides to the
finest courses of Great
Britain, Ireland and
now... Florida

Each *Golfing Gems* edition gives you
72 wonderful, sometimes lesser-known but
accessible, courses to play. Unlike other guides,
no charge is made to the Clubs for their
inclusion as entries are allocated purely on
merit. Color photographs and an extensive
editorial commentary on each course make
these an essential addition to any golfers
library.
Golfing Breaks is the only comprehensive
guide to the golf resorts of Britain and Ireland.
Many feature photographs of the course and
hotel, a description of the facilities on offer
and key information for the visitor including
local places of interest.

Look for them in all good bookstores.

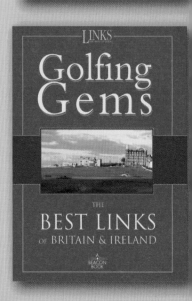